To every guy who has had a deep and profound impact in my life.
It is your influence that has shaped me on the journey to discern,
to create, to love, and to live out my authentic self.
To my amiable dad and my two brothers who are
not-so-little-anymore.
To my ~~future~~ husband.

Amaka is a living testimony of the saying that it is not what life throws at you, but how you respond to it that matters. She has learnt valuable lessons from the "school of life" . . . that emotions are no respecter of persons. . . that some experiences are non–negotiable. . . that at the end of the day, when your eyes are opened, what you see is a deeper reflection of who you are called to be. These experiences not only provide her with wisdom and valuable lessons, but also with the "sweet" credibility to coach (or to share, like she prefers) because she has been there.

Chinyere Distinguished Anoke
Author of Single, Friutful and Fulfilled and Turning 28

* * *

Our past is a mess of wonderful things and horrible things. The way we tell it at age twenty is different from the way we tell it at sixty. Every retelling of the story gathers more details of the blessings life brings and adds more weight to the BIG Story.

One of my closest friends, who is such a *pain in my neck,* asked me a soul-searching question the other day. The kind of day when a girl cries over some guy who broke her heart, or when she finds out she is not the only one in the picture. . . yes, that kind of day.

"So Amaka, among all these boys now, in all these your relationships up and down, which one was worth it ehn?!"

Wait a minute, what kind of friend would ask you that while you still have tears in your eyes and with your face looking like a hurricane-just-happened-here? Well, that's Chioma. Knowing how annoyingly persistent Chioma could be, I replied without giving it much thought, especially so she could stay off my ~~back~~ neck.

I said something that didn't really sit right with the pretty little girl in me. She didn't let me have it. She repeatedly made it clear that I wasn't only lying to my friend but I was also lying to myself . . . to God . . . to the world.

She repeatedly made it clear that I wasn't only lying to my friend but I was also lying to myself . . . to God . . . to the world. (Yes, that was intentionally repeated. Not funny, right?)

In that moment, it dawned on me that I had been withholding the truth. I had indirectly chosen to ignore this truth, or better still, not to face this truth. And it took me quite a while to finally look at the truth straight in the face.

I knew I could no longer ignore it. I knew it was what I wanted to tell and I felt it was time to bravely tell it. I wanted to share my story, not only to heal myself, but hopefully to also inspire others.

So I write. . . *He Wasn't My Husband.*

There are loves that just cannot be. Perhaps not. I don't know. At the time, it was pretty hard to tell whether God was trying to teach me something or life was just being mean to me. I'm just trying to make sense of all the times I had fallen in love.

After all, we're all just out there giving the wrong people a chance until we meet the right one. It's not like we can control how long that takes, right? So why should anyone feel bad for spending some time wading through all the people who didn't make it to the altar with them?

I write. . . for people who feel everything deeply and allow themselves to feel that way. I write for the people who believe in something hopeful; the people who are fighting to be better, fighting to heal, fighting to believe that they are worth fighting for.

This is me telling the truth. My truth. I am literally ripping my heart out open. I am letting it all out. Word by word, page by page, chapter by chapter.

This is not a story about pain, it is not one carved out of sheer imagination, fantasies or fairytales. It is, on the other hand, my true life story . . . the story lived through the very fibres of my heart. The heart which you will get to know as you flip through the pages of this book in your hands.

This is not a story of regret, it is not one shared for condemnation, pity or fear. It is, on the other hand, a life-changing story . . . the change which has inspired me. The inspiration which you will not be able to wait to share with your loved ones after you have read every bit of it.

Everything in this book is true . . . except that I've changed almost all the names and locations to secure identities for reasons that will become clear.

I'm learning so many things through this season of releasing. I know God's timing purposely corresponds with the writing of this book. Many emotions have swept over me during the last couple of relationships; but if you ask which emotion served as the common denominator, I would not hesitate to say rejection.

Be prepared for a massive flood of emotions.

You may smile, you may cry, you may get up to hug someone, you may sit laughing. I don't know for sure how you will respond, but respond you will.

I must warn you though, you are very likely to find yourself in it, lose yourself over it and find yourself through it again and again. And things might get really creepy.

Still and all, it's nothing to worry about. You will enjoy the experience, or should we call it a journey? Come with me!

With love,

Amaka

TABLE OF CONTENTS

Dedication
Preface

I LIKE GUYS. . .

PART ONE: THE GIRL
CHAPTER 1: What I Wanted
CHAPTER 2: My Background
CHAPTER 3: Peep into My Heart

PART TWO: THE GUYS
CHAPTER 4: Ben
CHAPTER 5: Chidi
CHAPTER 6: Jerry
CHAPTER 7: Enitan
CHAPTER 8: Farouq

PART THREE: THE REAL DEAL
(AS SHARED ON AMAKAMEDIADOTCOM)
CHAPTER 9: Dear Diary
CHAPTER 10: Dealing with Heartbreak
CHAPTER 11: The Healing Process
CHAPTER 12: Taking The 30-Day Man Fast

PART FOUR: LETTERS
CHAPTER 13: Letters from God
CHAPTER 14: Letter to My Future Husband
CHAPTER 15: Letter to My Future Son

THIS PAGE'S NOT THE END
One More Thing
Acknowledgement
About The Author

I Like Guys...

Yes. No. I mean, not really.

I can't say when it all began or when I first felt that loneliness, or should I call it emptiness? What I do remember is a point in time when I decided to forgo what I held dear. I remember the point when I foolishly thought, perhaps I was deceived into thinking, that I had been trapped by a self-imposed principle about boys.

Initially, the plan was:

I WILL NOT DATE ANY MAN WHO IS NOT GOING TO BE MY HUSBAND.

I wanted to save my heart. I wanted to. . .

But gradually, I started to loosen up.

The principle wasn't helping me find a boy, a boy to call "my boyfriend". Truth be told, how can a young-calm-beautiful--Jesus-loving girl find a husband without dating any man? Girl gotta ignore that principle!

The blocks on which the principle was built started to fall off layer by layer.

Then I became boy crazy!

I was curious to know what it feels like to have a boyfriend.

I kept myself open to possibilities - personality, distance, ethnicities, etc.

During my National Youth Service (NYSC) year, I saw (emphasis on *saw*) a guy I liked. Let's call him Gbenga. Gbenga was tall, handsome and muscular. He was so *foineee*. If I had a list of what I wanted my ideal boyfriend to look like, he checked all the boxes. I was helplessly crushing on him. I wanted him to want me. Luckily, we were both in the broadcasting team (OBS) at the NYSC camp. We hadn't talked one-on-one. He hadn't asked for my number. But I was so sure he'd ask me out somehow because. . . am I not pretty?

There were other guys like him — tall, dark and handsome — but I liked him the best. His voice was deep and hoarse but soothing to the ears. We were doing the same thing at the same place, announcing with a microphone. *Maybe he likes me too but doesn't know how to say it,* I thought.

Two times after I first saw him, I pulled myself together and set out to be the first to say "Hi". *What's the worst that can happen, anyway?* I convinced myself that it was a brave thing to talk to him. I decided within me to smile when he comes up with a good idea, or laugh when he makes a funny remark. I was going to shoot my shot. Yes!

I smiled my best smile. Hmm, I think I also gave a seductive look. Something like that.

"Hi?"
"Hello."
"You are in, erm, I saw you at the OBS studio."
"Yeah. I go there sometimes."
"I go there too. How are you enjoying camp?"

He seemed interesting and interested altogether. We had a good time discussing about the past and the present — memories back from school and memories back to where we were.

I didn't notice his nice set of teeth until his lips curved into a slow, heart-stopping smile. He smiled at me. Or rather he smiled with me. I could swear we had a connection there. I fell in love.

* * *

Another day, I tried to register what I had seen. Are they holding hands? What?

I felt sick to my stomach. I was sad. And broken. Weirdly, I didn't feel mad because I had no right to be. Did he ask me out? No.

I saw Gbenga talking to Sue, a girl I met at Oshodi garage. We coincidentally boarded the same bus to the NYSC camp, Ikare-Akoko. Sue and I became friends the moment I saw her big box and knew she was headed to camp like me. We just got talking and before we knew it, we were roommates sharing a bed, a bucket . . . and a boyfriend.

I hadn't made another new friend within the period. Sue was the only girl I talked and moved with. She was the only girl I had taken photographs with. As days progressed at the camp, we grew fond of each other. I had to put up with Sue telling me about her moments with Gbenga. The more stories she shared, the more uncomfortable I felt. I wanted to say something, but I couldn't talk. So I kept quiet. Sipping it all in.

Gbenga bumped into me at the studio some days after. Guess what he asked? "How is Suzan?"

How dare you, Gbenga??! No guilt. No shame. No remorse. He definitely saw nothing wrong in what he was doing to me. To my heart.

Of course, Sue must have told him she and I were bunkmates. And even if she hadn't, he had seen us together a couple of times. He knew we were close.

I became jealous. Very jealous.

If I can't have him, Sue won't. I was determined to break whatever it was they were trying to form. I didn't care. I saw him first. Met him first. And spoke to him first. Why would she want to steal my man?

One day, after the morning drills, as Sue and I strolled to Maami market, I expressed my feelings. I told her what I chose to believe. The truth in my head.

I should have said, "Sue, look I'm not sure if you knew that I really liked Gbenga. I'm happy to see you two are getting close, but please it may take some time for me to feel comfortable with it."

But instead, I said, "Sue, did you know that Gbenga asked me out? Well, I refused. So he came to you."

No girlfriend would want to hear that. No one enjoys being the second option. From that moment, Sue started to avoid Gbenga. Goal achieved. We both won.

* * *

Guys like Gbenga got my attention easily. They were my weakness. I was blind to how much I lusted after a relationship, how ravenous I was for love, and how much this one thing consumed my thoughts. My perspective had a long way to go.

I realized that, like many other girls, somewhere deep inside was a loneliness and a wish to have that special guy in my life. Sadly, I didn't exactly know what kind of a guy I wanted, who deserved me, and when I would be ready for the real thing. So I got attracted to some guys because of their physical appearance, behaviour, etc.

"Why do I get so attracted to guys easily?" Perhaps, you are asking yourself this question in this season of your life.

There are a few possibilities according to my assumptions:

- *Limited experiences: I* think this could be a considerable reason. Have you been involved in relationships with guys? If no, then this could be a reason. You, maybe, are curious about how it feels to be with a guy.

- *Maybe you see people (guys) flawlessly: I* mean there is a possibility that you never see the negative traits of a person (Guys, in your case) which is actually a good thing. That is why, you tend to see the only "good" in them and get attracted to them.

- *Maybe you are easy to impress:* Believe me! Sometimes there are some people who are extremely difficult to impress, and I guess you are not one of them. You are the kind of girl who falls in love after a small kind gesture from a guy.

- *Maybe you don't have someone special in your life:* I mean there are some times in life, when a person actually needs someone even if he/she has friends and family. That space can be fulfilled by only that special person.

- *Maybe you prefer the company of guys over girls: It* is very common for girls to prefer to be friends with guys rather than other girls. Reasons are many.

When I am in a relationship (using that term very loosely) with a guy who has progressed beyond a third or fourth date, but it hasn't been declared a relationship, I have no idea what to tell my friends I'm doing when I plan on hanging out with the guy on a given day. "I'm going to go have a drink with this guy I'm hanging out with," is totally appropriate, but so is "I have a date with *insert name here*" So, are we dating, or hanging out after the third date? Are we going to get married, or are we just having fun?
I get confused in between.

I usually end up saying I'm "in a relationship" with someone, even if it's been only two weeks since we've started going on extremely romantic dates. I just end up being the sad girl who didn't ask them to make it explicit or leave me alone forever.

I gave each guy second chances. Chances to show a girl what it feels like to have a special guy, what it means to be in a relationship, and what it means to love and be loved. And in the process, I found myself to be deserving of love.

I also found out that my quest for love was wrapped up in the need for perfection. Like many women, I'm a perfectionist. I live in a world that is constantly threatening my sense of balance. I desperately needed to feel like my piece of the pie – my body, my heart and my soul - is in order and stays-in-love.

By the way, Sue is now married and has a son. I don't know about Gbenga.

PART ONE
The Girl

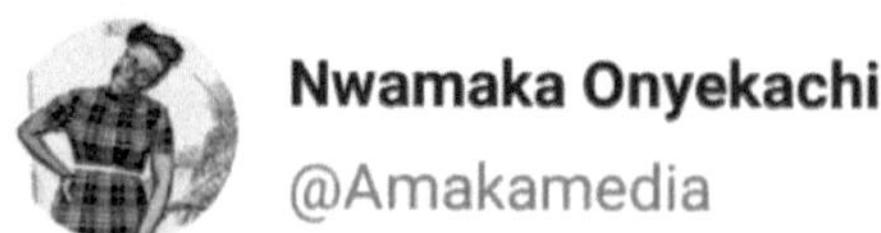

Nwamaka Onyekachi
@Amakamedia

A good girl is one who stands by what's right, just and true. Full stop.

8:11 AM · 22 May 14 · Twitter Web Client

CHAPTER ONE

What I Wanted

"Investigate my life, o God, find out everything about me; cross-examine and test me, get a clear picture of what I'm about; see for yourself whether I've done anything wrong — then guide me on the road to eternal life."
- Psalms 139:23-24, Message

I love great older women. And I wanted to be one. The easiest thing to do was to close my eyes and see me there. Being it. Living it. But when I opened my eyes, I could not believe it.

I have spent more than a decade and a half of my life searching my heart to know what lies inside of me, the human being that I am. It's not that I cared about what people thought of me then or now, but somehow God's spirit brings me to the point where I have to look inwards. I'm called to look within so I would find the answers to the many questions that arise in my mind.

During these times, I would always pick up my pen, get a blank sheet, and write. It comes like magic. And its magic is ever pure. Real. Surreal. Awakening.

After all these years, it finally happened to me. Maybe I should keep my eyes closed because I am not sure I am ready to face the next step. It must be heaven that I made it to because I do not feel any flames burning in my flesh or razor-sharp objects plunging into my body. But then again, I am dead and I no longer have a body. I am in a dream. All of the thoughts are racing through my mind and I can't do anything but write.

I grew up writing. I wrote everywhere and about everything.

Since I couldn't talk to save myself, writing became my safest and most comfortable form of expression. It became an art of talking with myself, with God, and with a best friend.

And in my writing, I bleed.

One minute ago, I thought I was fearless and now here I am, petrified to put the words together because I am not ready.

I was never ready for anything. I was never ready for eternal damnation in hell. I was also not ready to truly appreciate the perfection and the divinity of heaven if that was what awaited me.

Only twenty-eight years old and I already feel like I am living it, the statistics — one 30-year old woman who is not married. There is so much I wanted from life, but even more than I did not want.

I wanted to be married before 30. *Preferably* at 23.

Out of all the days, if this hadn't happened a few months ago, I would have been content, but not today!

Today, I feel I must have been on pills when I decided to write a book. Today, I worked on one paragraph for seven hours, after which I threw it away. Today, I cannot relate to or identify with writing a book that someone would like, let alone read.

Sometimes, I wish my journey was simple and linear so I can easily turn a blind eye to reality. To the facts I know too well. To the struggles I am trying to get through. But here I am, still trying to make sense of my journey and still very cautious because I'm not ready to break my own heart again.

What if I open my eyes and this is all just a dream? I will not fool myself. Not anymore. If I was dreaming, I would not feel so at peace. I would not be able to remember what happened before I went to sleep and I would be lying here wondering if I am dreaming. If I was dreaming, I would be so bloody scared when I open my eyes.

"Ahhhhhhhhh!"
"God. . . God. . . what is this?"

I'm speechless because never in my wildest dreams would I have expected to write this. I am crying out desperately, hoping to find an explanation. With the pen in my hand, I am bleeding.

Still bleeding.

Years ago, I bled so much that I had to spill out into the world. I started a blog. I started writing a series of posts, telling the stories of my life. Everyone has a story to tell. Sometimes, I wish everyone could have a blog the same way everyone has a Facebook account. It is a wonderful thing.

The blogging process encourages me to pause, stop and think deeper. I have been forced to delve deeper into the fabrics of my life and the threads that shape them. Through blogging, I learned to be more open, honest and vulnerable.

It's all coming back to me
Like the dew of the morning
It smells new and fresh
How I love this beginning
I sense it
I write again

I was rusty and maybe blind
Cos nothing seemed writing about
But today, I see everything
Everything is making sense
I see it
I write again

I heard sounds but didn't understand
I went where I couldn't be found
But now, I know where I am
Somewhere I can view things right
I know it
I write again

This feeling hasn't been lost
The smell of something fresh
Still lures me into this scene
Where the heavens allow me
The ink is flowing
I write again

I write again
I'm writing again
Yes, I write again

© 2014 amakamedia.com

I know I have some great stories, and there are people and emotions which haunt my mind that I would love to tell the world about.

My memory is coming back slowly. I have allowed myself to glide back in time, to re-enter each scene, I am going through the lanes to find the truth. To make a clear cut between reality and imagination. Again. All over.

I really do enjoy writing. And I have learned to love it even more over the past four years of blogging. But it can be mentally, spiritually and emotionally draining. Authentic writing includes your heart, soul, and mind. It calls you to tear yourself open for everyone to see. And emotional fatigue can be just as real as physical fatigue. Phew.

I keep answering my questions and digging deep into my beliefs and choices. It was first a habit, now it has become a lifestyle. A life where my intuition, a razor-sharp intuition, takes over and I have to make myself listen to it. I am digging deep into the abyss of self and soul. *Who am I really? What do I want exactly?*

I was always very hard on myself. So hard that I beat myself up. I have put some irrational and just plain crazy expectations on myself. I want to be perfect. I want to be exceptional. I want to be really good at everything I do.

I mean EV-UH-REE-THING.

I wanted to be:
- Somebody's wife
- My own boss
- A healthy woman
- A voice-over artist
- A radio presenter
- A true Christian
- A good friend
- A good Nigerian

I wanted to be all these things at once and at all times. I never wanted to be a writer.

I didn't know what was happening but I was compelled to write. I wrote and wrote.

And as I relived the memories, I could barely notice the tears slipping down my cheeks. Realizing. Releasing. Forgiving. Sharing.

One day, I woke up and noticed my right hand was trembling. I looked at it and saw the thumb and forefinger moving non-stop. I had no idea why but I assumed it was because I had committed putting my butt in the chair and writing — no matter what.

Sometimes, maybe all we need to do to find our calling is to see what's always been there. Now that my eyes are open, these are what I can clearly see:
- A scared little girl. . .
- An angst ridden teenager. . .
- A bemused young woman. . .
- A newlywed wife. . .

A Scared Little Girl

I had, I think, a very wonderful childhood.

I came full of hope. I took my first breath. I smiled for the first time, and the whole wide world actually lit up. I was born into a life I knew nothing about, a world I never knew I would come into. I had to be here...

TO GIVE MYSELF. To be naked. To be vulnerable.

The sweetest gift, the only gift I could give is ME. My presence. My fullest truest presence. Anything I was, anything I am and, anything I will be. My path had been prepared. I was to take on a journey. A journey for which I have been born.

I learned to sit. I sat. I learned to crawl. I crawled. I learned to stand. I stood for the first time, then I fell. My legs got stronger. Soon enough, I learned to stand on my own. I took my first baby step.

I learned to walk. I walked, I fell, and then got back up again. I continued to walk and walk. I was not stopping . . .

I jumped. I danced. Oh, I loved to jump and dance.

I opened my mouth. I made sounds that could not be put into words. I screamed. I screamed out of pain, yet out for joy. I spoke my first word, "Ya". I was told it made my dad happy because at the time, he'd lift me up and say "*Ya*" as he catches me. Every time I said "Ya", I was certain that my dad would carry me up. I enjoyed it.

I'd like to think ya means yes. I said yes to laughter. I said yes to love. And I said yes to life.

Life is an amazing journey to discover who I am. And to discover the fullness of who I really am, I have to embrace every experience and discover the lessons contained within those experiences. I have to learn from them. Grow. Evolve. Become.

Becoming isn't immediate and neither is life. Both need to be nurtured over time and allowed to move in unexpected ways. People, events, things provide me with opportunities to discover who I am and what I want.

The world will be what it is. The events will happen. People will do what they do.

As a child, I felt and experienced emotions. I could tell if you are happy and relaxed or tense and upset. I was aware of the people, emotions expressed around me, and the environment in which I lived. I experienced happiness when my dad got me chocolates, anger when my mum refused to let me go out and fear when. . . Fear? Lots of it.

IS FEAR A NORMAL THING?

I read that every little girl is afraid of something. Some don't like the dark. Some don't like loud noises. Some don't like strangers. Others hate nightmares and scary movies. And then there are those who want to run away from mean dogs, snakes, and creepy crawly things.

Me, I was afraid of everything. Abnormally afraid. Horrendously. Shockingly.

I was afraid of the dark. I was afraid of the sounds at night. I was afraid of being alone. I was afraid of creepy creatures. I was afraid of Father Christmas. I was even afraid of dolls. Yes, dolls. Baby dolls. All kinds of dolls.

I'd rather use a sweatshirt to create a baby doll that I could play with than have the one bought from a store. That thing scared the hell out of me. Some had fixed staring eyes that were akin to those of a corpse or a witch. Maybe it was my imagination.

Whenever I was scared, I would come with full force and start demanding support and attention from those around me. Surely it was up to my mum, my dad or the next closest person to make me feel better. My parents thought I was possessed of an evil spirit; they couldn't explain my actions. My tears. My fears. My voracious need for attention.

I craved attention. It was my soul-food.

When I wasn't given the attention, I would throw in a tantrum.

I played with my dolls made with sweatshirts and fed them when they cried. I was going to be a good mother. A great wife. A lovely woman. I just knew.

I have always imagined I would get married one day. The dress, the chapel and the elaborate planning have never appealed to me, but creating a home with the person I love and opening myself up to that level of intimacy and commitment, does. I viewed marriage as a creative and serious life endeavour; two people coming together and building a shared life they can both thrive in as individuals.

I wanted to grow up. Fast.

An Angst-Ridden Teenager

My hormones started to build up. Puberty hit me. My body started to change. I had never felt this way before. Suddenly, I started to feel like a stranger. . . a stranger in my very own body. I didn't understand what was going on . . .

I felt something good was happening inside of me. Sometimes, it was so painful that it made me cry. Sometimes, it was so sweet that it made me bubble with joy.

The distance between the who that I needed to look like and the real me was so wide that the only thing I could do was to drive myself harder and harder, until the day I gave up and ran the other way.

Another alternative was to stop running, and to actually ask myself what is real here:

Is it true that I am fat?
How fat do I think I am?
Am I really fat? If I believe that I am fat, why do I believe so?

I didn't like what my body was turning into.

The truth of false self-identity is that it evokes memories of never being good enough, of feeling awkward. At this point, my identity was in a fragile state.

It was hard being a teenager; it was confusing and tough.

There may be no end to dealing with the longing to be like who I want to look like; it would perpetually depend on what I am going to do about it. I can work with it, speak about it. Or, I can live with it. There is no end. There is no cure. There is only a relationship and a willingness to enter into it every time it called me. To look and see who I am, and how I identify with myself.

I mostly battled with low self-esteem and poor body image. I didn't like that my thighs were thick. I didn't like my teeny-weeny voice. I didn't like my brown teeth. I didn't like the image I saw in the mirror.

I was an intelligent teen who came top in class but I wasn't a confident one.

I was quiet, introverted and incredibly shy (this shyness hasn't been totally wiped away though). My shyness wasn't just about being afraid to talk to people; it was also about not being able to fight for what rightfully belonged to me. I was painfully shy. It still hurts to think about how many opportunities I missed.

My shyness was also as a result of placing too much focus on myself.

"What do people think of me?"
"Are they looking at me?"

"Would they laugh at me?"

Building confidence had to be a process. A process of developing self-acceptance and self-love. It wasn't just going to happen. I had to DECIDE to get away from myself. I had to stop worrying about what people thought of me. I had to take control of my thoughts. My confidence. My life.

* * *

The process started to happen at age 16. I was in my first year at the University of Nigeria, Nsukka.

We were grouped into tens. Based on the first letter of my surname (at the time, it was *Ajaegbu*) I was among the first set of students to present the GSP102 class seminar. I still don't know why the members of my group chose me as their major speaker. Could it be that they saw my future-self addressing a large crowd? Because I don't get it!

The lecturer called *Group One*, so we all stepped out. And the pretty shy me mounted the platform.

If only they knew my inner struggles. I was nervous. Anxious. Uncomfortable. Scared. Uncertain.

My body was shaking so bad by this time and my mouth felt like someone shoved a whole pile of cotton balls in it and stuffed them deep down! Then I noticed that not only were my hands shaking uncontrollably but my heart was beating so fast and hard that I could hear it. My inner thighs felt rubbery and out of control too. I recall my right thigh was trembling so much that I tried to hold it down with my hand just to stop the movement my leg was making!

Oh my! I'm freaking out here, I thought.

"If you have nothing to say, you can as well go and sit down and let others talk!" the lecturer snapped. I forced myself to look at her. I can still remember what she looked like. She was a short fair woman with a black bob weave, wearing chunky earrings and bangles. She wasn't smiling. I wasn't expecting her to, anyway.

I looked at my teammates whose eyes were fixed on me as though their lives were in my hands. Well, so it seems. An 'A' in a course worth 10 units would have a huge impact on their GPAs. Their eyes were pleading for mercy. They were begging me to save them.

Oh, okay. Okay. . .I thought.

I just have to prove to everyone here that I prepared properly for this moment. Alright, alright!

Deeeeeeep breath.

Their noises jolted me back to reality. The claps were echoing.
I did it!

I spoke so well that the lecturer suggested I change my department to the
Mass Communication department because she believed I was born to be a
speaker.

I couldn't believe myself. The shell in which I had hidden broke.

My life changed in that moment.

I realized I could do anything. Be anything. Whatever I wanted.

I was determined to stay out of my shell, and I was like a debutante
coming out for vengeance.

They said the best vengeance is self-love and acceptance. I wasn't only
coming out for that, I was out for love and acceptance from boys. It seems
to be almost a rite of passage for teenagers in some ways.

The best word I can use to describe my first encounter with love is
awkward. As far as the feelings I experienced, I remember the nerves, the
tingling sensations, what you call "butterflies". Yeah, it may sound sappy
and cliché, but those things really do happen to people the first time they
think they're in love. For me, it was definitely the case.

He was the first to tell me I am beautiful and that he liked me. He told me
things every girl would crave to hear. His voice had a wild and calming
effect on me, like he had a spell on me. My heart raced, like a glow in my
chest, every time I saw or talked to him. Time was only mine with him. I
will stop it, replay it, and rewind it a zillion times. That feeling was
awesome. That feeling when there are butterflies in your stomach, that gets
you into feeling like you are not in the present world. That confused and
excited state. That feeling that gets you jumping and dancing all over the
place. I felt all of it.

Ah, young love!

The feeling of being in love for the very first time is perhaps the most freeing, exciting, and terrifying experience — all at the same time. When he moved away to another state, I was devastated. It was an early lesson for me about the beauty and power of opening my heart to another, as well as the awareness that opening often comes with a closing that can feel harsh and unfair.

A Bemused Young Woman

You are never the same person after you have fallen in love.

Until you've lost a love that you built up to be the kind of sappy fairytale that'd make even Cinderella jealous – until you've lost the person who you thought you'd wake up with every morning 'til one of you dropped dead – you'll never understand what it's like to be truly crazy about someone. Crazy enough that, even when they've moved on, you can't accept it and let yourself do the same.

I was a confused young woman who couldn't move on from all that consuming I-love-your flaws, I-love-your-heart, I-love-everything-about-you kind of love. I compared every new tall-dark-handsome guy that crossed my path to my old love, and no matter what the new guy did, he never measured up to the massive ghost of past love that was haunting my heart.

I was messed up. I was broken. I was losing my mind.

In trying to find my mind, I made myself emotionally available to every Ben, Chidi and Jerry. I was pretty much an open book. I found it easy to be vulnerable and let a guy get close to me because I was hopeful it would lead to love.

Of course, it didn't take long for relationships and heartbreak to ruin all that. It never feels good to be vulnerable with someone who doesn't reciprocate. It never feels good to stay open for love when you've been disappointed one too many times. Whether it was out of insecurity, bitterness or cynicism, they weren't giving back the same measure of affection I was giving them. I was a discontented young woman.

Why can't they love me right? Why can't I find true love?

I didn't want to give up on finding love. I was extraordinarily optimistic when it came to relationships.

I cried; I starved; I fasted; I prayed.

If the definition of a date is a pre-arranged meeting of two people with the purpose of seeing whether they're compatible, then I think I dated over 15 guys and fell in love seven times. Several times got me close to the altar but something always happened. Out of those seven loves, I would say four were magical, mostly overwhelming to the point of losing myself. I mostly stepped out of the things that mattered to me.

I didn't know better. I wanted to give all of myself to the person I loved.

That is just the type of love that flows through my veins. I give it my all.

Getting over a heartbreak was the hardest thing. I almost died. I still wonder how I didn't die. Oh, my heart. Every time I start to get over a guy, I'll run into him at the bus-stop or somewhere or I'll have a dream about him. It was rubbish. Absolute rubbish.

I was constantly tired. The fighting, the drama, the weeping — it was too much. I couldn't sleep. I felt like I would never be enough for another relationship.

I became the obsessive, pathetic, crazy, prepossessed ex-girlfriend. I was a young woman who couldn't let go – and who would never admit it to anyone else. Not even to her closest friend . . . usually, not even to herself.

I couldn't move on, completely. I needed help. I needed healing. I needed to be made whole.

My journey to healing started. . .

Yolanda Adams' song, *Fragile Heart* was my favourite song back then. I sang it a million times. The lyrics made sense to me like it never had. You should listen to it.
With tears in my eyes I prayed like:

"Lord, my heart aches and pierces me. This pain is too much for me. This pain is too much. It's too much to carry, Lord.

I prayed that He would fix everything people broke in me. I prayed that He would erase every person who came into my life and left holes in my heart. I prayed that He would just cleanse my heart and rid it of all the mess, all the chaos, and all the heartbreaks.

And God being who He is heard my cry. As I gave Him my broken heart, amazing things started happening. . .

Healing can be painful and messy. It's like having an operation done in your heart, seeing it go through the cutting and washing process. An author once described the healing process as "walking through cleansing fire." I guess it is an accurate description. When the journey starts, it can feel a lot like tearing the mask off your face and tearing your heart open.

But nothing is as painful as staying stuck somewhere you don't belong. Once you've decided to move on, there should be no turning back.

My journey to healing was actually a long stretch. I took three steps forward and two steps back most of the time. One repentance never seemed enough. I needed a large dose of it. I struggled. I pleaded with God;

"God, forgive me!"
"Help me!"
"I'm so sorry!"

Yet every step of the way gleaned new understanding. There came the realization that every stumble and setback was worth it, because each path brought me to my knees, to God and to my truth.

Nobody will ever understand the pain a woman who was once in love goes through trying to be whole again without that special guy. All this woman can do is trust God and hope that, someday, she'll fall in love again – if not with another man, with herself, or with the God who loves her silly.

And someday, she will love and be truly loved.

A Newlywed Wife

Sometimes it still doesn't feel real. I'm a wife. I now have a husband. Just how?

The plan was to have this book published as a completely single lady. I wanted it to be some sort of conclusion for my season of singlehood. I wanted to boldly declare that I did not hold myself back from doing what I am supposed to do with the pain and heartbreaks I have experienced. I knew that the pain of being criticized or judged for my book will be nothing compared to the agony I would feel if I didn't write it. It seemed I was taking the leap of faith to get to the end of my singlehood and say, "Goodbye Singlehood. Hello Marriage!"

I literally had no idea I would be married by the time this book would be out. I really *really* wanted to finish this book before getting married. But here I am, asking my cute husband, "Baby, which is better? To reveal that I am married at the beginning of the book or to reveal it at the end?"

My marriage is such a plot twist. I am still marveled at all the many (and wonderful) changes that took place between the time I thought of writing *He Wasn't My Husband* and the time it got to the printer. Wow.

It all happened within a year. A proposal. A courtship. An engagement. And a wedding.

Oh, wait, it actually didn't happen within a year. God set me up for a decade. I have long been prepared and set on a path towards the person I wanted to be. Somebody's wife. Kachi's wife. And at just the perfect time.

I just might write another book to tell the story of how I met Kachi and how we got to the altar to become man and wife, because it appears this one I am now writing can only serve as a prelude.

Oh my gosh! It still feels like a dream.

I was as single as a slice of bread, still living in my parents' house, copywriting full-time and keeping fairly busy. And in the twinkle of an eye, I BECAME a wife. I feel different. Forget it, marriage is a life-changing experience. Is it the sex? Is it the cooking? Is it the inside-jokes? *So much more than I have ever imagined!*

I never dreamt marriage could be this much fun! I've been adjusting incredibly well. So far, there have been no major surprises . . . except that my husband burnt the first set of eggs he wanted to fry for us to eat together. The eggs turned black! But guess what? We ate them just that way. While he was good and fine, I ended up visiting the toilet over and over again. We still laugh about it.

Becoming a newlywed is a game changer.

What has changed? Everything. And it's the FEELING of being married that has been a complete game changer. I am yet to get used to being addressed as Mrs. Onyekachi. Fortunately, it's a nice surname (meaning *'Who is greater than God?'*). I like it.

We are still adjusting to saying "husband" and "wife", and this man is constantly obsessing over his new wife and fidgeting with the reality of me (which is the definition of adorable). In the middle of a discussion, he'll smile (or sometimes hit my buttocks) and call me "Omalicha Kachi" (which means the 'Kachi's Beauty'). When I am dressing up, he'll give the hmm sound and call me "Omalicha Kachi" or coyly say "My wife, my wife". Then I'd chuckle. Don't ask me what happens afterwards.

The two of us are having so much fun. We laugh more than ever before. We love exploring our new experience together, eating breakfast, (sometimes) lunch, and dinner together. We eat too many eggs. We eat plantain a lot. We drink too much water. We take so many photos. We share everything except toothbrushes. We make a mess at dinner time and clean up together. We stay up way too late — watching movies, talking, and laughing about the goofiest things. We love those special times of sharing our highs/lows and praying together before bed. Our goodbyes are long, and our hellos are even longer. It's a joy to be able to say goodnight at the end of the day instead of goodbye. Weekly fasting is still a priority, and we look forward to them. On weekends, we love going out for a great time and having a long nap.

I am still filled with awe every time I think about the fact that while I was writing *He Wasn't My Husband*, God was busy writing my love story. Maybe His own title had been *He Is Your Husband*, who knows?

Future is an unknown place but for now, I will keep my head up, believing wonderful things await me. One thing to always remember is, we can get through things. We can be happy. We can reach our happily-ever-after. We can get to the point where reality becomes better than our dreams. We can. We will.

~Love Still Here~

I waited for love
That it should come
I imagined it to walk by
For I stood there
Wanting love to find me

I started on my way
Engrossed with my doings
While I was working, walking
It appeared like I felt something

"Who is that?" I asked
I expected a baritone as of a male
Or a soft tone as of a female
It wasn't exactly what I imagined
It came roughly, dusty and rusty
But I saw the shape and recognized it

It was love.
I knew it was love from the start
That beautiful day we met
So I found love
Or perhaps love found me
We've been together ever since
With love still here

© amakamedia.com

CHAPTER TWO

My Background

"Tell me, what is it you plan to do with your one wild and precious life?"
- Mary Oliver

"Excuse me boss, you have a text message. . ." That was Daddy's phone ringtone for incoming text messages.

The phone rang that morning while we were having our devotion in the sitting room. Mummy, Junior, Nnamdi, Chibuzor (a cousin who was living with us at the time) and I didn't think much of it even though we all heard it. We just thought it to be one of those casual text messages. We continued. Undistracted.

After the last "Hallelujah" for that morning, we all left for our rooms except Daddy who stayed back with his phone.

"Adadaddy, come!" Daddy called out. I could sense some level of excitement in his voice.

"Yes, Daddy?" I came out of my room eager to hear the next group of words from his mouth.

"See!" He handed over his phone to me, with a confused smile on his face.

My heart was racing. Anxiously, I looked at the phone. It was the text message that got in while we were sincerely praising and praying to God.

I took a deep breath and sat down. I read it again. And again. I didn't even realize I had been standing the whole time.

The text read:

Congratulations! You have just won N1 million. . .

I can't remember the rest of the text message but the first six words already summarized all that were needed to know.

"Eh!" I shouted.

"Don't shout, we are not sure yet." Daddy was skeptical.
"Junior, Junior come and see oh! Daddy won one million Naira."

Junior couldn't get what I was saying because I was talking with
excitement. My voice has a tendency to be high pitched and sharp, like the
squeak of a mouse in your cupboard when I'm giggling with excitement.
My words were not clear.

"What happened?" Junior asked.
I gave him the phone and pointed for him to look at it.
"Yeh! One million Naira from MTN? Like for real?!"

Nnamdi and Chibuzor ran into the sitting room. Both of them stood
staring at our smiling faces. "What happened? "What happened?"
"Daddy just won one million Naira!" I announced to them.
We were all jubilating, dancing and singing.

Mummy walked in and asked indifferently. "Which one million Naira is
that?"

* * *

According to the text message, Daddy would have to go online - I mean,
log in to a website - to get a pin code that would qualify him to claim his
prize. Going online meant going to the cybercafé. We didn't have access to
the internet at the time. But how time flies. In those days, very few people
had access to the internet except those who had VSAT or those working in
big corporations. Interestingly, today, people don't go online anymore
because everyone is always online. All you need is an internet-enabled
mobile device and the world is (potentially) yours to conquer.

The verification process required us to visit the cybercafé that day. Junior
and I decided to go there together. As we logged in to the website, we saw
the faces of happy people; some had placards with the sum of one million
Naira written on them. We looked at each other and smiled.

"It's real o! It's real o!"

As we typed in Daddy's phone number, we got a notification that a
verification code had been sent as a text message to my daddy's number.
Hurrah! We walked back home happily. Junior and I were discussing
about what we would do with our own share of the money.

"*Eh!* My laptop is so sure."
"Now I can change this fake phone to an original one."
"Millionaire's daughter. *Ghen-ghen!*"
"With one million Naira, our level will change."

When we got home, Daddy had left for a meeting or something. Only Mummy, Junior and I were around.

"How far?"
"It's real," we told them.

From that moment, everything and everyone began to associate with the word *millionaire* in the house. A minute didn't pass without millionaire being mentioned. *Millionaire's Daughter. Millionaire's Son, Millionaire's Wife* and *Millionaire Everything* became the order of the day. We made jokes about it. It was a big deal for us.

It called for a celebration.

We were all in the sitting room, munching chicken that night while watching *Who Wants to Be a Millionaire* on TV. We loved that quiz show. Many times, we would answer the questions for the participants correctly, and wrongly a few times too.

Power went out. "*Eh!* NEPA!"

"What are we going to do with our N1million?" I asked immediately, as though I had been waiting for power to go out.

"Don't count your chickens before they hatch," Nnamdi said with chicken in his hand. There was something about his expression that made everybody laugh.

"Yes! It's true. What are we going to do with the money?" Mummy supported me.

Before anyone could say a word, Daddy answered, "I am going to buy a car!"
Our mouths were left agape and our ears stood. *What? A car?*

We didn't expect that that would be the first thing on his list. Daddy didn't have a car. He had never driven one. That day, I realized that Daddy had a dream of owning a car.

"We can't get a car now. We have not built our house yet," Mummy reasoned. Till date, she believes getting a car doesn't make business sense. Not everything in life needs to make business sense, but Mummy always think about cars in that category.

Junior made a similar remark but Daddy protested.

O boy! What would I say now? To get a new car or to get a new house? I thought to myself. I, like Mummy, saw a car as a liability and a house as an investment, especially when the house has a freehold title. Land can appreciate over time but cars don't. The moment you drive a new car out of the dealer's shop, its value basically halves. More so, a car has ongoing maintenance costs that need to be factored in.

"See Daddy, as an accountant and one who has studied inflow and outflow of cash, I would say that it is not financially wise to get a car. . .a car is not our priority now. . ." I went on and on.

"Alright! Not now, but I must get a car," Daddy retorted.

We agreed.

Mummy, who had not said what she would want to get out of the money since Friday, finally ~~said~~ recited all she ever wanted. She wanted a gas cooker, a new wardrobe, and a good sum of money.

Junior, Nnamdi, Chibuzor and I including the millionaire himself also started declaring what we would want to get out of the one million Naira. A new generator set. A new home theatre. A new dining set. A new mattress. A new wardrobe. A new laptop. A new phone. . .the *new* list was endless.

"Well, till tomorrow," Daddy concluded.

We had planned to go online to claim our money the next morning.

Then the morrow came. We mentioned the money in our devotion. We asked that God's will be done.

So Daddy and I went to the cyber café. Our eyes glued to the monitor.

We were filled with anticipation as we filled the e-forms. Daddy dictated while I typed.

It was all fun until the box popped up:

Insert your ATM PIN here

"It's not real," Daddy whispered.

My heart broke.

I was beyond disappointed. Puzzled. Shocked. Confused. I didn't know what to say.

No genuine portal would request information as personal and private as one's bank account Personal Identification Number. It was a fraud attempt. I couldn't cry.

Although we had gone to the café with a level of certainty, we were not fully convinced but quite optimistic. If you were in our shoes, wouldn't you have had a little hope?

Here we were. Our little hope of having one million Naira had been dashed. It was a scam. Now, what was going to happen to the endless list we had been talking about all weekend? The generator set and the home theatre and the new dining set and the mattress and the wardrobe and the laptop. . . and everything that had been attached to one million Naira in the house?

"I guess we'd have to forget about it," Daddy snorted.

Forget about it indeed.

Well, I didn't. I captured the memory and kept it safe in my diary. It's not easy to forget about something that made you upset. It's not easy to forget about something that made your stomach turn. It is not easy to forget about something that made your heart pound 50 times in a nanosecond. It is not easy to forget something that broke your heart. It's not easy to forget.

The ups

The downs
That's life

The light
The dark
That's choice

The love
the hate
That's living

It will come
It will go
That's the journey

© Amakamedia

My upbringing is of a unifying one. We worked and prayed together, nurturing our love to keep it positive and in full force against any opposing force that tended to tear down our family unit. We are a very close family woven together by difficult times, learning from our experiences and following peace.

I was born into a family of five:
My daddy
My mummy
Me
And my two not-so little-anymore brothers.

Daddy

The earliest memory of my daddy that I remember was when I was three years old. Before he went to work, he would just talk to me. Sometimes he would cut my nails, very delicately.

Daddy fondly calls me "Adadaddy" meaning "The Father's first daughter". Like most little girls, my father was my first love. I adored everything about him, even how he smelled (like beer sometimes). The sound of his voice on the phone still makes my heart skip a beat. Some of my happiest childhood memories involved listening to his stories about how he struggled with my grandfather just to marry Mummy.

I've seen my dad laugh, worry, pray, complain, shout, praise. But I've
never seen him cry. The only time I saw him close to tears was when he
hugged me and told me how much he loved me and how proud he was.
He looked me in the eye and said, "Adadaddy, I am proud of you! Thank
you!" I had just won the RedStar Scholarship at the time.
Ah, priceless moment.

If a girl gets that affirmation and approval from her daddy every now and
then, she is not going to be desperate to get it anywhere else because she
already has it.
I wanted to see Daddy proudly smile about my success again. I wanted to
earn his approval. I wanted him to look at me and say, "I am proud of
you" again. I wanted to repeat the moment. But it never happened. It
turned out to be just another memory. . . a memory that cannot be
forgotten in a hurry.

Choosing my fondest memory of my daddy is hard because there are too
many. One of my favourites is when he told me to dress up in the dress he
had just bought for me. That particular evening, he took me out to dinner
and treated me as if I was a date. Looking at his face that evening made me
want to pray to marry a man like him. He showed me what to dream about
my marriage.

I dreamt of a man who would treat me like Daddy did. Like a princess.

Daddy never forced me to do anything I didn't want to do. How could he
say no to me? I was his only little princess. He paid extra attention to me.
And was even more protective of me.

Daddy probably could have been more emotionally involved. "Toughen
up," he would say. He didn't want to talk about icky stuff like boys, sex,
sexuality and relationships.

I was not allowed to have a boyfriend. I was not even allowed to bring a
boy home. If I did, I'd be frowned at or spoken to as though I had
committed the biggest crime ever.

I never brought any guy home to meet my dad until I was 22.

Actually, no. Not really. I didn't know that he was going to be around
when the guy visited. So accidentally, the guy met him at home. So yeah, it
was an unintended introduction. Quite awkward.

I remember returning to campus after a long ASUU strike. I was leaving home very early in the morning with a big box and a Ghana-Must-Go bag. Daddy didn't have a car to take me to the park. We couldn't get a cab. Daddy carried my big box on his head. As I watched him, my heart cried. I wrapped my hand around his muscular forearm and stroked my fingers gently along in silent gratitude. I was, and still am, thankful that he is a vital part of my life.

I became determined to make enough money so I could buy him a car. Daddy deserves the world.

Mummy

This book is actually much more about the men in my life; the ones who left and the ones who stayed. But how would I sleep at night if I didn't mention Mummy? How would she be happy and proud if I didn't write a page about her?

I came to be because of Mummy.

I guess it was a bit tiring. It must have been really tiring for a baby to come out in the world. And it must have been hard to come to Mummy who was the only person I knew. After a long rest and a few months in the warmth and comfort of her womb, I was born into this brave new world. I was unsure of what to do with myself, or even what I really was.

I'd like to think I came out of my mother's womb as every normal child would. Mummy's womb was dark, cozy and warm altogether. When I got out into the brightness of this world, everything was so strange and I began to cry out, "Where am I? Help!"

Suddenly I felt something holding me. I felt my mummy's warm skin and the constant thumping that seemed so familiar to me. I heard her heartbeat. My cries began to subside as I felt comforted by her embrace.

I smelled something enticing, colostrum. *Yummy!* And I began to root around for it.

This delectable scent reminded me that I was hungry and would like to eat, but the umbilical cord attached to me all those months was no longer doing its job. Suddenly I felt Mummy's nipple pressed against my lips and I began to open my mouth. At first, I was clumsy and I fumbled, not sure of what I was doing. But there was something instinctual in my movements and I felt it at the time, that it was the right course of action.

Mummy helped to guide me and then I latched on to her nipple. *Hmmm, the sweet nectar!* The liquid tasted just like what I was drinking in the womb all those months. I felt an instant comfort in the familiarity and then I was at peace. Ah. This is home.

Mummy was my first teacher.

Literally. She taught me.

She taught me how to eat. She taught me the alphabet. She taught me how to read. She taught me how to spell. She taught me to be a woman who wakes up very early in the morning to make food for her family. She taught me to participate in activities at church.

Mummy did not only teach me that food is good for the body, she also taught me how to cook good food. But I didn't want to learn. I was not that kind of daughter who loved the kitchen. I was not a foodie. Still not.

Being a non-foodie doesn't mean I hate food or that I cannot cook o. I cook. I have no allergies, I'm not a picky eater, and I can eat pretty much anything called food. What makes me a non-foodie is just that I'm not someone who gets excited about food and its process of preparation. I'm not keen on following food reviews and blogs. The latest food trends or latest restaurants don't matter much to me. And I don't take photos of my food from a creative prompt to post on social media.

While I cooked, I couldn't wait for the food to get ready so I could leave the kitchen. Mummy kept saying, "How would you cook in your husband's house? Don't you know you are a woman?"

And I kept wondering whether I would be a good cook. I was not sure anymore. I started praying for a man who knows how to cook. Daddy cooks well. Growing up, I saw him cook when he wanted to. In my mind, having a husband like Daddy was the surest bet for a girl like me. In my prayer, I also added:

May my husband enjoy cooking for me.

It's one thing to marry a man who can cook, it's another thing to marry a man who enjoys cooking. I wanted both worlds. (My next book would tell you what I eventually got.)

Mummy is a teacher - has always been and will always be. She worked as a teacher in a government primary school, and as a Sunday school teacher at church. I believe she was born to be a teacher. She is so passionate about sharing knowledge and telling others about the Word of God.

I remember the day Mummy asked me, "Is there someone?"

Her question startled me. Mummy had always talked to me about school, work, career, church, parties, hair, God and avoided issues about relationships with boys. At that point, I figured I had gotten to the point where I could proudly bring a guy home. So I told her I was seeing someone.

Naturally, she was curious. "Who is he?" she asked.

"Well, he is a comedian," I said.

Then, I showed her a photo of us, to which she nodded politely. She thought about it for a moment before she turned to me and asked, "Where is he from? Do you like him?"

Wow.

Mummy is really interested in my relationship?

She no longer saw me as a child. That conversation brought us closer together.

Emotional discussion must certainly be an important step towards improving communication with a mother. We moved closer to that strong, connected, mature relationship we've both been hoping for. I could tell her about anything. We could discuss our fears, triumphs and pain. We could cheer each other on Facebook. We could laugh together and even gossip about the boys living with us — Daddy, Junior and Nnamdi. The next time she asked me, "How is he?"

"It didn't work out."
"It is well," she comforted me.

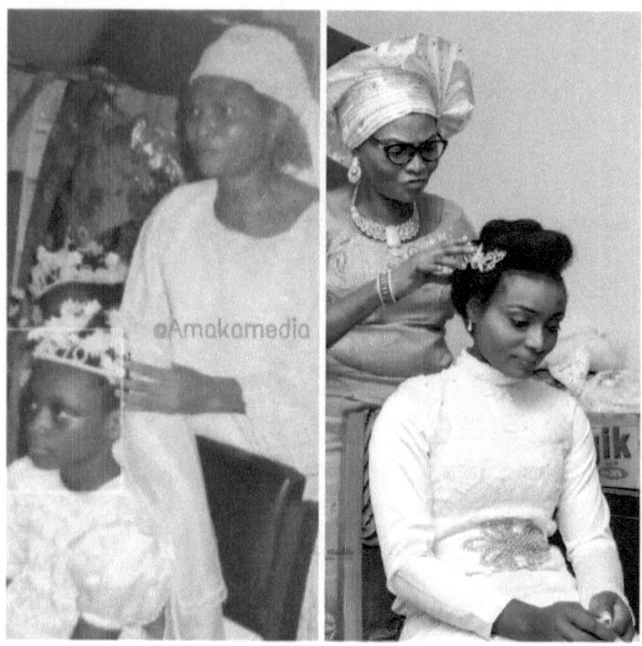

Mummy has always been there. We lived through some very difficult times together. Despite everything, we are still very close. Mummy has my utmost respect and admiration for her perseverance through hard times.

My younger brothers:
Davidson Jnr. and Nnamdi

It's amazing how a girl can love her two brothers dearly and want to wring their necks at the same time.

As children, my brothers and I had a rocky relationship. We spent the better part of our childhood fighting. Daddy did not want to know and would stay out of it. His attitude was, ignore it and it will go away. We got on better when he wasn't there, so he believed that any hostility between us existed only because we were warring for his love and attention.

I think it is the responsibility of parents to make sure siblings get on as well as possible. Some parents don't help, either by over-involvement or absence. However, my parents tried hard enough to hide which of us were their favourites. *Thank God!*

Mummy regularly told the three of us — my brothers and I — that she desires us to get along when she leaves (leave to where? I don't know), to support and love one another along life's path. We are, I believe, granting her that wish. Right, bros?

My first brother, Junior is three years younger than I am. He is intense too. I love him very much. And I have the greatest respect for him. Sometimes I feel as if he is older than me because he has quite an advanced view about life. He believes, like Neil Gaiman, that life is a game; that life is a cruel joke, that life is what happens when you're alive and that you might as well lie back and enjoy it.

Junior has had a past where he did crazy things, but that has changed. How did he change? That's a surprise to the family. He constantly surprises us. He has strongwill power, and will achieve the goals he sets for himself. He knows what he wants and will never take no for an answer. If he doesn't like or agree with something, you will know.

Junior acts more mature than the rest of us. His level-headedness thrills me. He is my motivator, he really is. For a long time, he told everyone that his sister has a blog. He proudly announced himself as my PR manager. He got back from work one day and asked me:

"What happened to your blog?"
"What happened?" I knew what he meant.

I'd not blogged for days. It was very unusual for me not to blog for that long without a cogent reason — few times were when I lost my phone and when I needed to reconnect with Jesus. Whenever I knew I was going to have a busy-ness week, I'd always schedule my posts ahead of time. However, that season came along with a different cloud of rays.

"I don't know what to write." I responded without even thinking. My very own words shocked me because I never even realized the TRUE reason for not posting until then.
Junior said nothing. But the silence was loud.

"Thank you for asking. That means a lot to me," I said shortly after.

He gave me a nod.

"Why don't you write about why you don't know what to write?" he said, as he turned towards his room.

"Hmmm!"

He meant it as a suggestion. But I took it as divine revelation. *I should write about how I feel right now.*

Now, whenever I get stuck, I just call Junior and he is always ready to build up my confidence from level zero to level high.

As kids, we fought a lot about silly things but today, we have bonded so well. There is no love like the love from a brother.

My second brother, Nnamdi, who is seven years younger than I am, is the opposite of Junior. He falls under the category of adventurous if you ask me. He is the one brother I feel closest to because he is a funny guy who is always ready to act as a lunatic just for the fun of it.

Nnamdi can see things you won't see and present them from an angle that will make them hilarious. Funny guy. He has the kind of laugh that you would want to record and play again because it is soothing and pure. Nnamdi is not the kind of person who swims against the current. He does his own thing and is never really worried about what other people think of him.

I don't know how he did it but he outgrew all of us. He grew taller and bigger than the rest of everyone in the family. A big teddy bear. We tormented him and my mum always said to him, "Stop eating too much so that you will not blow up". Eventually, it happened. He reduced the amount of food he consumed and started exercising every day. He became a model guy - tall, slim, cute, muscular, nice, sweet.

I would describe Nnamdi as high-maintenance. He needs the latest model of everything and he only gets the best. We both have this repulsion towards the conventional way of living. The *Nigerian mentality* is something we can talk about for hours in disgust, pointing out all the faults and pressures that falling into the trap can do to our dreams. Nnamdi is a dreamer too. We support each other's dreams and ours is a relationship I would never want to lose.

You know what. When I was growing up, I cried to my parents to give me a sister. I'd say, "Mummy, Junior can say he has a brother and a sister, Nnamdi can say he has a brother and a sister. I can't say I have a sister. When will I have a sister?" I really *really* wanted a sister. It took me years to realize that my parents gave me one of the greatest gifts of being a sister to those two big boys. It's the same thing as, if not more than, having a sister. What was a sister going to call me anyway?

Sister. Isn't it?

That's what my brothers call me already.
It's amazing. I am their sister. Their only sister.

What would a sister do that two brothers can't? What's the good news if they have no sister to share it? What's the use of a large wardrobe full of shirts if they have no sister to wear them?

Friends come and go, but my brothers stay. No matter how many times we get on each other's nerves. No matter how many times I get annoyed with them about something they have said or done. No matter how many times we have said things that we regret, we always get over it. We are family. Always will be.

I must say this, it's wonderful to be and to enjoy the full benefits of being the only daughter. I wear Mummy's clothes and carry her handbags. I wear my brothers' shirts. I get extra cash from Daddy. I get the biggest room. There is no sister stealing my clothes. Oh, it feels great! Yes, I am pleased to be the only girl in the family. The only sister. . .the only princess. . . who had to bleed to become a queen.

Growing up with two boys certainly had an impact on the woman I grew up to be, and I will always be thankful to them for that. They gave me a chance to be a big sister, a teacher, a wife, a mother, a role model, but most of all, they gave me companionship.

And I'm thinking, people who didn't grow up with a brother or two, how did they cope?

Just asking.

CHAPTER THREE

Peep into My Heart

"Above all else, guard your heart, for everything you do flows from it."
- Proverb 4:23, NIV

My heart is a big one filled with many emotions.

It is both a blessing and a curse.
I had a hard time letting go of the ones I should let go of.
I had a hard time cutting off from the ones I should have released.

The problem was my heart.

My heart gave the same second chances over and over again. My persistence didn't allow me to give up so easily on my relationships, even when they seemed impossible.

I would stay strong for months and then out of nowhere at 2:00AM, I would sit on my bed crying out a river.

My biggest defeats were gained because of my heart. And my biggest blessings, my heart as well.

My heart gets in the way. In my way.

The major part of all my struggles was how my heart reigns over my mind.

Well, maybe I was no different from every other girl you know. In my opinion, a woman is an emotional being. She is indeed a fragile creature, set to love and serve someone, someday. When I love, I love hard. The romance becomes something seen on screen in a fairy tale movie.

Despite my calm façade, I experience every emotion of all caps. Unfortunately, because I love deeply, I can become quite possessive which leads to mood swings. But these mood swings are not bad.

They simply show I really care about the person I am with. It might take a while to get used to and understand my mood swings, but once you get to know me, you'll love me.

Back then, I was gullible. I tended to assume the best in everyone, and it's often not the truth. I also tended to believe most of what was said to me, but could still be suspicious and reluctant sometimes.

Today, I carefully choose who I let into my world. But once you are in, you are in. Consider yourself blessed. I am in it for the long haul. I will stand by you through thick and thin. I'm not only the friend who will listen to you cry. . . I'm the friend who will cry with you.

I do not trust easily. No matter how I let you into my life, I still maintain a level of mystery. I find it difficult to open up to those who do not personally understand me, and most times don't even bother trying.

I may appear cool and calm. However, I can be quite the opposite. It depends on the hour because my mood seems to change like the winds.

There are many sides to me. I am made up of many layers and it's hard to put me into one box. Just when you think you've got me all figured out, I will go and do something totally unexpected that you never saw coming. I surprise myself too. Don't judge it to be a split personality disorder though. The side you see (or should I say get?) depends on the depth of our relationship.

I may appear extroverted, but no. I am extremely introverted. (The truth actually is, the Spirit in me moves in extroverted ways).

I am overly sensitive and deeply passionate beneath the surface. I am extremely intuitive. Those who know me well can see past the tact to my passionate (and sometimes moody) inner self.

My sensitive core leaves me with a vulnerable spot, and I am easily hurt. Blunt words can cut deeper than intended when spoken. I have to try as much as I can to avoid confrontations. Confrontation is not just a threat to my balance, it creates the perfect forum for the blunt words to strike my heart. I wish people would speak only to lift others up — whether it is gossip, criticism or unkind remarks. But then again, people will always be people because their mouths will always move. *Phew*.

Confrontation is my worst nightmare. It's been hard to deal with that. When it seems inevitable, I react by shutting down completely. I retreat back into my shell and regret ever letting my guard down in the first place. Any hint of criticism and you are likely to find me withdraw, begin to sulk or dissolve into a flood of tears while refusing to talk about what went wrong.

When I get into one of my legendary moods, it is entirely up to me how long it will last. No amount of prodding and provoking will make me emerge from a self-imposed retreat. I will come back to you when I am ready and not before that.

Since I'm a very passionate and sentimental woman, you'll have to flatter me, talk to me gently, and show your affection towards me with words, and actions.
I overthink a lot of the times, I come up with conclusions, and I even act upon them. It's better to be straightforward and honest with me all the time to avoid any misunderstanding.

I constantly needed reassurance so that my insecurities wouldn't get the better part of me.

My need to feel assured in love can also give way to fits of jealousy during which I build a wall around myself, give in to brooding or go into a self-pity mode.
Despite being very sensitive, my heart isn't as fragile. The opposite, I keep on going in front of any setback, and I come out stronger. My Spirit provides me with a gift - the one of always finding a way out to continue my path, whatever obstacle I face.

Again, just because I am emotional does not mean I am weak. When I feel like I am being used, I will not be afraid to let go, regardless of how much I have fallen for you.

I was quite easy to date (well, I like to think so). I love places that are intimate and romantic (like the beach, waterfalls, etc.), with no loud noises or food that is too spicy. I like the crowd, but I prefer it more when the crowd is made out of people I know. The best thing a guy could do was to surprise me with common sense, adventurous points of view and amazing treats that he is so sure I'd like. He could surprise me by making me happy. *Not too much to ask for. Is it?*

Oh, I just remembered when one of the guys I dated said that one of the challenges about dating me is figuring out what I really want. I laugh about it but now I think he was right.

Because of my deeply emotional nature, I had always expected him, as my boyfriend, to be in tune with my secret wishes and desires. Like if he asked me where I would like to go on a Saturday night and I say, "I don't know, you decide", it is my way of telling him to refer to all our conversations over the last two weeks and glean the part where, in a small voice, I may have mentioned an antique shop tucked in a quiet part of the town that I have always wanted to browse through. I love it when the one I love listens to my unspoken words and hears my quietest wishes.

I am the kind of woman who puts her heart into everything.

I learn new things faster and do things better when I have a personal connection with them. I mean, if something does not come naturally to me, I would not want to take the time and effort to make it work. Thus, if the relationship is not magically falling into place, I will bail faster than you can say "Check please!"

For me, love is like a living being, someone I should dedicate my time, my attention and my love to. I knew that every detail counts and that is why I always think and focus on the particular guy in my life. He consumes my entire thought. My heart. My being.

In my past relationships, I have discovered, I was the most romantic. I enjoyed dedicating my time and love in the creation of a bond that kept gaining consistency from the beginning, and that kept on growing as time went by. I am capable of pouring out all my innate creativity to improve the pursuit of a lasting relationship.

I am a dreamer, loving and thoughtful.

I am endlessly imaginative. I literally have the craziest and silliest ideas. And the best part? I act on it! Yeah, you heard that right. I will go to any length to chase my silly ideas and make things work. I prefer to think deeply about things rather than simply take everything at face value. And that, I must say, can also be my undoing.

I have a knack for seeing my imaginations come to light and if they don't, it sometimes feels like I have failed in life. When imaginations become fantasies, then there is a problem.

Imaginations are not all bad and one has to understand the power of imagination to appreciate the concept. It is bringing into perspective by spiritual sight the desires of the heart. Sometimes, Heaven places these imaginations in me, but the flesh does too. So I struggled with casting down imaginations.

And I have always lifted my eyes to the hills for help. Constant help is needed to lose, smash, crush and destroy all patterns of wrong imaginations, wrong ideas, wrong beliefs and wrong attitude.

Only God can change this heart. He is the only who can see things about me that no else can see. Deep things. Hidden things.

One time, He showed me the content of my heart and I gasped. It was a hard pill to swallow. Gosh. I blogged about it. Here's how I put it:

I have not been feeling very positive and inspired lately, so I decided to visit The Healing Centre. When I got there, it seemed the Doctor knew I was coming. He had already opened my file and was treating my case. He said I'd be needing a surgery. Whoa!

One thing I love about My Doctor (and Heart Keeper) is that He treats me as if He feels my heartbeat. Or what can I say? He gives me the impression that He knows what I feel every time I feel it. So professional, yet so personal. I've never met anyone like Him.

I peeped into the file (bearing my name) on His table. And I saw what had been recorded:

Symptoms

Anger
Heartbreak
Death
Depression
Emptiness
Fear
Loneliness
Loss
Pride
Unforgiveness
Restlessness
Uncertainty

Weariness

Lab Tests

- *What is happening on your altar - is the fire still burning?*
- *How many people have been drawn to God because of you?*
- *When people seek to harm you, do you respond with such kindness and love that would shock them?*
- *Are you still in love with God or you just love the idea of Him?*
- *If you still act any way and anyhow you want, are you truly a Christian?*
- *When a friend asks you for advice, do you answer in the flesh or in consideration of the word of God?*
- *If God answered all your prayers, would the world look different? Or just your life?*
- *Is your goal to be married, or is your goal to fulfil purpose in marriage?*
- *Are you going after a dream you want or the God who instilled a dream in your heart?*
- *You can claim you be a Christian, but are you producing the fruit of the Spirit?*
- *Is your goal to be known or to make Him (Jesus) known?*

Test Result
HIGH EXPECTATIONS. LOW PATIENCE.

Drugs/Medications
Dwell in His presence
Read the Bible
Be still and know that He is God
Stay calm

Surgery Required
Let her heart be opened
Remove her heart as it is poisoned with pride and pain
Give her a new heart; a heart like Jesus

Bottom line: Our Heart Keeper knows us better than we know ourselves. And He sees those issues within us that no one else come close to seeing. Yet He still loves us even with all our conflicting desires and imperfect follow-throughs.

Sweetie, when was the last time you had your heart checked? Hurry. Run to The Healing Centre now!

* * *

It's humbling when God keeps scrutinizing your motives and your hidden intentions, especially the ones you never knew about. The heart is where the REAL deal had to happen. It had to be broken open and filled up with God.

Since then have I been perfect? No. Do I still struggle? Yes. Have I fallen? Many times. But His love never lets me go. He keeps changing and transforming me.

When you begin to see how lovely you are, a God-loving heart arises within you. You become fully aware of God's love. Your heart becomes so full of love that you start spilling it all over the place. You would crave to give a creative expression to your heart's content.

I started something called *Heart Rays*. I tagged it "light from the heart" as an expression to spread positivity, inspiration, and love.

I didn't sit down saying "It's high time I changed people's lives! No!" I was a hot mess at that moment in my life. The last thing I had any business doing is saying "Hey! Now people, let me give you the answers."

I do not know it all and I doubt I ever will, but I was committed to sharing from my heart based on what I have lived and believed. I was also looking for grace and resurrection in my own life and it ended up helping people. *Amazing stuff!*

It has been long accepted as a fact that creative people work with their hearts, and are more likely to be depressed, obsessive, anxious, suicidal or schizophrenic than the rest of the people in the world. Although this has not actually been proven true but I want to believe it's true in my case.

I can be dramatic. One scene can unfold a thousand other scenes in my mind. One minute, nothing matters more than this thing I just created. Then minutes later, I am more than willing to throw it away. Throw it all away! For instance, I say in the middle of my writing, "This sentence has to be the most beautifully written sentence" while labouring intensely over it. I love it when I read it but then when I read it again, I realize it doesn't work at all.

I have referred to my creative work as my baby when in actual fact I have
been its baby because everything I am and have become is from the
creative things in my life. They were making me.

I didn't have *Heart Rays* as a project. It had me as a project. It was creating
me. Not the other way around.
As I was doing it, I was becoming it, and I was loving it.

In the heart, there exists a her
A being as the feminine nature
Appearing in the finest vesture
That the king may long to have

In the heart, you will find art
An expression of life in styles
Creating beauty for the eyes
That the tale may tell its part

In the heart, there is a song
A tone of pain, of joy, or of hope
Reaching for the very aim to pop
That the time may not be long

My heart, again will hear
The sound of music in it
Living on rhythms so sweet
That it may say, "I belong here"

© *amakamedia.com*

At the end of the day, the things that matter are the matters of the heart.
All a woman like me wants is a life filled with love, comfort and stability.
Even when she seeks reckless adventure, she yearns for a sense of security.
She craves the sensation of feeling safe in a place she can freely call her
home.

PART TWO
The Guys

Nwamaka Onyekachi
@Amakamedia

50 years from now, people are going to ask me what my biggest setback was in life . . . I'll look sternly in the camera and say "boys".

1:59 PM - 7 Mar 2017

CHAPTER FOUR

Ben

"Never settle with anybody that treats you like you're ordinary."
- Unknown

I wouldn't say I didn't see you coming. I certainly did.
Yet. I. Let. You. In.

Ben, you came into my life like a hurricane, sending me late-night texts, proclaiming your adoration for me, even though I had only hung out with you in a group setting.

You were almost never found talking with girls; I was the only girl you had interacted with in the group.

I liked the way you talked. The way you walked. The way you carried yourself. The way you held your audience with such ease was admirable. You were a born-leader. You were funny. Not the canny kind of funny either. You revealed a sincere sense of humour that even cracked up the older men. Your personality was too large for this little girl; I barely contained your laughter.

You were a real charmer — essentially, everything I could have wanted in a guy, right down to a pair of amazing cheekbones (Ladies, don't underestimate the power of defined cheekbones).

The way you carried on a conversation drew me in immediately. I enjoyed spending time with you. You gave me all the attention. I was comfortable in your presence.

And here's the thing: we meshed so well. For the first couple of months, we were constantly laughing, cuddling, watching movies, and tangling up the sheets. We had a total blast. By the time I knew it, we had been together for over two and a half years. Until that moment, your faults seemed like perfect imperfections that I found endearing.

There was the waiting and the fighting and the times when I thought my heart would break into two thousand pieces. I made excuses for you, so many that I fought for you time and time again even though you probably never deserved it.

When I look back on it now, I think the only problem was you. You weren't ready for my love. For the things I was willing to give you. And that's okay.

As I write, I ask myself why did I fall for you?
Was it your looks or what you had?
You were not as tall as I want my man to be
Neither did you ever spend a dime on me
Even if you lose everything, I would still be there for you.
Your love would be enough for me
But you didn't love me . . . like that

And it took me quite some time to realize that.
I could have left so much earlier.
I guess I just didn't want to admit it...
that whatever it was, it was just "it" for you.
Never meant more.
Nothing more.

I could sit and wait, but it would hurt more when it's time to leave.
So I asked you,
"Do you want more than this?"
"I can't"
And that was enough for an answer.

Your intentions were obvious. The way you adjusted so seamlessly from our time alone together to our time outside the world. You invited yourself into my life, blurring the lines between Friday and Monday. My guard quickly dissipated as you made yourself a stable fixture in my Sunday routine.

I didn't realize it at first, for this I will take the blame.

How It Started

He got my jokes and I got his. We laughed so hard together. Over time we enjoyed each other's company so much that he didn't want to leave the church premises. "I don't want to go home" was something he blurted out when it was time to go home. He liked me. And I liked him too. Our kind of relationship was rare and we were going to have a very special connection that some married couples don't have.

"I like your kind of person. Apart from Funmi, you are the only one who understands me." He knew the right words to say. He drew me in gently. He never said he loved me. Neither did he ever say he would marry me. But he never stopped saying how much he enjoyed talking with me, laughing with me, playing with me and just having me around.

He complimented my clothes, my voice and my hair. He knew how to make me confident when I doubted myself. I was in love with him before I knew what I was into. And when I knew, I was already hooked by his charm.

He asked me to promise him one thing, "Do not get possessive."

And yeah, I agreed to that.

I asked him to promise me "No sex." I wanted to keep my hymen for my husband.

And yeah, he agreed to that.

Then I asked him to promise to let me know when he gets a girlfriend.

Sure, he agreed to that too.

That was how our relationship which had no title, no direction, and no purpose was birthed.
He became my secret. My secret sin.

Memorable Moments

Memories. All I could do is relive my memories with you since we wouldn't be creating newer ones. And the memories of two years would last me a lifetime.

Mutual Lust

"Come here, Amaka."

My eyes closed against the surge of arousal I felt at the authoritative tone. Gosh, Ben smelled good. His body radiated heat and hunger, spurring my own wild desire for him.

I wanted him. Badly.

But he was no good for me. Honestly, I could screw up my life on my own there and then. I didn't need any help towards the path of destruction.

"Free yourself."

His lips brushed behind my ear. One of his hands was pressed flat on my stomach, his fingers splaying to urge me back against him.

He was as aroused as I was, his cock hard and thick against my lower back.

"Are you sure you want to do this?"

Disappointed and regretful, I turned in his grip. I was already led into the temptation, no deliverance nearby. He had set my body on fire. Hell felt sweet.

I felt helpless. *"I can't help myself,"* the voice inside of me whispered. I was about to betray myself.

Ben curved over me, his forearm dropped against the curve of my hip, tightening reflexively and driving me wild. Mad. Crazy.

"Kiss me," he said hoarsely
"I can't."

He ran his hand over my lips. "Kiss me," he repeated as though he didn't get my declination.

I was weak to my knees. I began to crave his touch like a drug.

"No, please," I snapped.

Something stopped me. It definitely wasn't me.

<u>For The Last Time</u>

I crossed my arms. "Let's just get this over with. I don't want to see you anymore."

Ben covered his eyes with his hands and exhaled harshly. "You don't mean that."

I was suddenly very tired, exhausted from fighting myself over him. "I really do. You and I . . . it's not a good thing."

His jaw tightened. "It's not."

I stared at him, startled by the fierceness of his acceptance. That was too direct. I was stunned. "I knew it was wrong from the beginning. I don't know how I agreed to this sort of friends-with-benefits deal about us."

"Do you want me to date you?"
"No, that's not. . ."
"Come here."

My heart started to pound. He didn't let me finish my sentence. I was going to tell him that I didn't want us to keep doing it. I was going to tell him that I was sick and tired of being sick and tired of the bittersweet feelings. It was an adventure for life but it was killing me.

He left the bed and came closer. "I want to be with you."

I stared at him, trying to figure out what he was about to do and where this was going. "What do you want, Ben?" I asked softly.

He caught me to himself and cupped my cheek in one hand. "I want you. I want to keep feeling the way I feel when I'm with you. Why do you want to leave me?"

I placed my palm over his heart and felt its pounding rhythm. He was anxious and passionate, and that had me on edge. *How was I supposed to respond? Do I go with my gut or my common sense?*

"What do you like about me?" I had already lost my mind.
"You are smart. You are beautiful. You are different."

The rush of delight that swept through me was ridiculously powerful. I loved his description of me. It was okay for me to see myself through his eyes. I wanted him to reintroduce me to me. I wanted to hear more.

And when I got back to my room, the truth behind his words came back haunting me.

You are stupid. You are ugly. You are not different.

I cried.
Again, I cried.
How do I get out of this?

It Was Her. The colleague

I was sipping *Farouz* and obsessively checking my phone, waiting for a text from Ben, who claimed he would call me when he got back home. Normally, I'd get a *ping* at the bus stop, telling me he was horny, he wanted me, sending me silly ideas he discovered, checking on my day plan - just sweet words connecting across junctions. Today, nothing.

It had been the same deal with the weekend before. That night also, no text or call - just oppressive maddening silence and no response when I called or texted. The dots started connecting.

And oh, one time, he tried to spark up a fight. Usually, when we fight we won't talk for days and even weeks, only to get back again as though nothing ever happened.

My synapses fired and my brain roamed in a direction that I tried to roadblock. Ben always, always had his phone in hand. His devices, be it laptops or phones, were always charged. Always within easy reach. It defied logic that now, his behaviour had changed.

I got up and took a bike to 17, Illesanmi Akanni street, Orile. I marshaled my courage, told myself the truth was better than self-delusion. I went straight to his room; his laptop was switched on and his phones, on the bed. Luckily he was outside washing his clothes, and didn't know when I got in.

I checked his phone, viewing the *missed calls, dialed calls, received calls.* My name wasn't there. But somebody else's name had been more consistent, Oluchi. They've been talking for hours, days, weeks.

I panicked.

I dialed my number on his phone to see what happens. It didn't ring on his phone but it was ringing on mine.

He came into his room and found me holding his phone. He was startled at first, then he shrugged. I pulled back to search his face, but couldn't read his expression.
I blew out my breath in a harsh rush. "Who is Oluchi?"

"Huh?"

He pissed me off by throwing his head back and laughing. The full, throaty sound flowed over me like a rush of warm water. I rubbed my face and saw a different thing. His amusement made him less than perfect in my eyes. I saw a demon. A Yoruba demon.

I felt like someone just stabbed me.

I was so numb.

I was so grossed out that he shared with her what he shared with me. I was scared, stressed, nervous, sad, dejected, what not. I couldn't sleep, read, pray, do anything. I kept asking him questions because I just couldn't understand. He couldn't even answer them.

I didn't leave immediately. I gave him a million chances to even make the smallest effort to fix things, but it was clear he wasn't interested in fixing things, at all.

I fought for him, gave him options, asked what he wanted.

"Choose. Do you want me or do you want Oluchi?"

He didn't know.
It was over.

Yet I stayed. Even when he said, "I love you, Amaka. But I can't marry you."

He told me Oluchi was whimsical and free-spirited; she didn't want marriage. Maybe, just maybe, I had to accept some of the responsibility for the straying, because what we shared had gone astray as well. But, h*ow do I move on?*

How It Ended

It was complicated. I think we broke up like five times or so.

We were in a skewed relationship. We were more than friends but less than lovers in a committed relationship. What we had was beyond a friendship and less than love. I think this kind of relationship was stronger than the other because in this, we didn't judge the other person. We didn't expect anything from them. It was totally selfless and eternal. But what about the future?

If a man says he can't marry you, but still admits to love you a lot, it's wise to ask him the reasons. Maybe he thinks you are not compatible; you could talk about it and address his doubts and fears. Maybe he is commitment phobic - maybe you can talk about taking some time. Whatever it may be, if he is transparent about his feelings and lets you into his apprehensions, doubts and fears without beating around the bush and wavering unnecessarily, he is probably telling you the truth. You will know, depending on the relationship you share with him. If nothing can be done, accept that some relationships are not just meant to be.

In any healthy relationship, you talk, no matter what. Ben and I were not talking. I went from seeing him two times a week to texting him once every two weeks. I started 'texting him because he stopped communicating with me. No texts. No random calls. Nothing. I was doing the texting and chasing.

I'd miss him so bad and text him, telling him I missed him and I wanted to see him. He wouldn't even at least lie to me and say he missed me too. One time, I lost my phone and I used my brother's phone to call him. He was the only one I talked with and I hadn't had any proper communication with my friends except for him. So suddenly, I didn't have a friend anymore. I was alone.

I'd text him once every two or three weeks. He would just keep quiet. I'd go to his room randomly to visit him, the way we used to. The conversations would be awkward.

I was miserable, but I cared too much. The problem was, I called him out on this at least five times, and each and every time he'd say, "You are my friend. Just don't end things with me. What do you want?"

And my response would always be, "Your attention. And our friendship back." I'd loved our friendship, so I'd sometimes suggest that we end things and just be friends. In response, he'd say he liked me way too much to just be my friend.

He'd text me the following day only, and disappear afterwards. He'd refuse a break up, but then continue to ignore me.

My heart was broken over and over during that *relationship*.

I was in a dark place, a very sad and dark place. I began to chase him again; I was desperate to have him back. He was like a missing piece of the pie. I texted him and called him, hoping he would want to rekindle, but that unfortunately led to a mountain of rejection.

Each time he rejected me, my heart breaks again. But maybe it hurt less every single time because the cracks were already there. Maybe I was expecting it. Maybe I was prepared for it, the times.

The breakup was hurting; the pain was traumatizing. It was tough to get through the anxiety, rejection and pain. It took me nearly two years to get over him.

I finally stopped fighting for someone who was just a shadow of a person, an outline of what could have been.

Lessons Learnt

I tried to focus on some of the clarity I received from him rather than the disappointment and emptiness I felt at losing the rare person who had felt like my personal person.

I still can't believe I was able to surpass my pride and forgive him for everything. I still can't believe he changed me. I'm thankful that Ben paved the way for me to know who I should be with, the kind of man I should look for, and what I want out of a relationship. I'm thankful for the lessons he taught me.

1. Develop Self-Respect

When you are in a relationship, you can either gain self-respect or lose it depending on how you allow yourself to be treated. Relationships are the best places to learn where and how you need to respect yourself. I learned you do not do anyone any favour by allowing yourself to be taken advantage of. I learned what my limits are and I acted upon those limits by asserting myself when I have been hurt.

You don't ever have to tolerate people who treat you poorly. It doesn't matter if it's a friend, a family member, or a partner. It doesn't matter how long you've known them or how nice they might have been to you in the past — you are allowed to set boundaries about what you want and what you are not willing to tolerate. You are allowed to vocalize how their abuse makes you feel. You are allowed to share those feelings and experiences with other people. And if necessary, you're allowed to leave and distant yourself.

You have every right to stand up and say, "I love you and I really want you to be a part of my life, but I can't continue to allow you to treat me this way. So if things don't change I am going to have to cut you out of my life. Not because I don't care about you or respect you, but because I care about and respect myself."

Self-respect perhaps forms the keystone of how we treat ourselves and how we allow others to treat us. When you have self-respect, you will know what you deserve and how you should be treated, when to walk away from someone who is not right for you and when to let go of someone who does not meet God's standard. You will know your worth and you will know that you want a relationship that makes you grow – emotionally, spiritually, mentally, etc – and a relationship that is worth your time, effort and *heart*.

2. Attachment is Not Love
We confuse love all the time and the media doesn't help. Everywhere we look, we're encouraged to accept attachment (or infatuation or enmeshment) as love – but it is not.

Attachment is motivated by insecurity.
Love never is.

Wanting (or needing) constant reassurance is not love. Jealousy is not love. Poor boundaries are not love. Fear is not love.

Attachment is toxic. It's being OK when you are with that person. It is not being able to live without them.

Love is beautiful. It is being OK without being with that person. It is not clingy.

Sometimes love can turn into unhealthy attachment, and sometimes it's never actually true love in the first place, just an addiction that you can't shake or have no interest in shaking. Unhealthy attachment are formed when you are willing to abandon your own interests to become overly interested in the other person's.

3. Virginity Is Not Purity

Ben and I actually discussed our boundaries: **no** sex.

But the temptation to further explore our bodies was constant and the pressure was great. I was alone, ashamed and had no one to talk to. I was so confused because I still had my virginity. I grew up in the church and so many of the teachings on purity were about being a virgin for your husband. So, why was I so consumed with the shame and disappointment as if I had had sex?

I never understood the value and meaning of my purity until I freely gave it away.

In my mind, I always thought I would never do more than kissing before marriage. Just like all temptations, when we flirt with it for so long, it is only a matter of time before you do something you never thought you would do. The more I did it, the more I wanted.

I let Ben touch me in places that belonged to my husband. Lies of the Enemy bombarded my mind. I became more concerned with the question, "How far is too far?" rather than understanding what God meant by purity.

Sexual abstinence is good, but purity is NOT defined by your abstinence. It goes all the way back to the heart of the matter. Purity is the attitude of our heart, responding with a heart of obedience, with right motives, and acting from a place of holiness (and wholeness). Before you were kissing, before you were holding hands, before you were flirting – what were your intentions? What were you thinking about? What were your desires?

Most Christians love the already defeated game of, "How much can I get away with and still be a Christian?"

Even though I maintained my virginity, I gave away my purity. It became clearer to me that my actions were not acceptable to God's standards. It became clear to me that I was delaying God's promises. It became clear to me that I was in a battle, and I had to fight. . .for my purity, for my peace, and for my *promised* future.

4. It is OK to Cut Negative People Out of Your Life

For some Christians, this is a hard concept to grasp and they will continually allow an untrustworthy person to remain in their lives for fear of being unholy. I get it, they turn the other cheek to be slapped again, right? No, no please! Relationships are built on trust. But when you determine that someone in your life cannot be trusted, is it really to your advantage to keep them close?

If someone has taken actions that prove themselves untrustworthy, believe them. People will show you who they are. Remove them from your life before the harm becomes irreparable.

Showing love and respect to others does not mean you should forgo loving and respecting yourself. God wants you to live in freedom so that you can positively impact the lives of others for Him. Make yourself as effective in that role as you can be by freeing your life from people who hold you back from doing so.

I made sacrifices for Ben, sacrificing even my relationship with God.

If someone's behaviour is harming you and their actions indicate that it will continue that way, cut them out already.

5. Imbibe Self - Acceptance

I needed Ben to validate me; my sense of self deteriorated when he wasn't giving me the attention. What I didn't realize was that I was giving away my power and putting my happiness at his mercy.

I made him my happiness. Unknowingly.

The truth is, if you aren't happy with yourself, you won't find that happiness in a relationship either. You have to cultivate self-love, self-acceptance and happiness in your life first, before you can share it with another.

Nobody can validate you.
Nobody can tell you your life's purpose.
Nobody can tell you who you are
Nobody can understand you for you.

You must make sense of these things about yourself, by yourself and for yourself.

Ask yourself these questions:
- In what areas am I most critical of myself? How does that make me feel? Does it ever help me rise or is it just keeping me down?
- In what ways am I unloving towards myself? What alternative behaviours can I choose to demonstrate that I truly do love myself?
- How do I reject my true self by pretending to be someone I'm not so others will love and accept me?
- What am I doing because I think others want me to do it, not because I think it is the right thing to do for me?

Whenever you feel yourself moving away from self-acceptance, choose instead to align your actions with what you know deep-down, in your heart of hearts, is truly right for you.

Before I could identify a guy and truly know the purpose for our relationship, it was important to learn to love myself.

Leaving Ben, the man I had long attached my heart to, was gut-wrenching. But what kind of woman would I have been if I stayed?

Nwamaka Onyekachi
@Amakamedia

Cute guy: Hi

Me: What's ur last name? I need to know if it sounds good enough with my name & the baby names I've already picked out for us.

11:01 AM - 21 Oct 2016

CHAPTER FIVE

Chidi

"Time passes, memories fade, people change but the heart never forgets."
- J. M Darhower

Chidi, your name woke me up one morning; I found my lips forming your song before I was well back into my body out of my dreams. I wondered if you were a tree where my spirit was nesting. The other night, you were a high tree and I was inside it, and the wind was gently blowing on both of us . . .erm, forget the rest. Whatever that dream meant, it was enough to make me wake up happy.

I can hardly remember anything about that night. The dreams faded when I opened my eyes. I saw the light. It illuminated the walls and daylight was too strong for the night to remain.

Oh, how are you? Are you awake? Up? Out? Have you eaten? I ask you so many questions. You never answered my questions anyway. You ignored them. You looked as though you were thinking about the perfect response but you were pretending. You said nothing. You disappeared.

Chidi, why would you leave me without saying goodbye?
Why, Chidi. Why??

How We Met

I was a first year student and he was in his final year. I was sitting behind after fellowship. We were waiting for the meeting with first years to start. Someone tapped me on the shoulder, I turned around and there he was. He said, "Excuse me, are you Mercy's cousin?"

Out of surprise, I blurted out "Yes!"

Mercy and I are cousins who happened to gain admission into the University of Nigeria, Enugu Campus the same year. We attended the same fellowship, although I was more committed than she was.

"Seriously?" he asked. He didn't seem to believe me.

I rolled my eyes.
"Wow. You guys don't look alike."
"Well, we are cousins." I shrugged.

Then he turned away. That was it. He only wanted to know whether Mercy was my cousin. I didn't think much of it.

I bumped into him once in a while. We talked here and there.

Shortly after I graduated, we started seeing each other more often. We lived in the same city.

He told me he liked me. Always had. From first year. He told me how much he loved the way I packed my natural hair for the Christian campus fellowship reunion that year and how he never stopped gushing about it to his friend. I could tell he was a sincere, genuine and easy-going guy.

"I liked you too. In fact, I had a crush on you," I said. And that was the truth.

~Mr. Man~

It's a bright, lovely and peaceful day
Here comes Mr. Man from nowhere
He walks like a boss, "Not bad"
He looks good, "Nice one"
I can feel his aura from here
He smells really nice, "Hmm!"
I'm thinking already, "Is he the one?"
I better put this thought away
He probably belongs to someone else
How blessed is the woman who has him!
"Wait! Why is he looking at me now?"
My heart is racing at an alarming rate
Butterflies in my stomach are waking up
I'm not so sure I like this feeling
"Look away from me!"
Mr. Man seems not to hear me
He is walking towards my direction
"OMG! Is he. . . is he coming for me?!"

Memorable Moments

Chidi was the kind of guy who makes a good girl go bad and a bad girl go good. He was a professional boyfriend. Yeah, he earned that title.

Seminar Date

It was a Saturday. Chidi and I had a date.

His plan was that first we'd attend a seminar. Second, we'd go see a movie. Third, we'd talk at Mr. Bigg's, one of Nigeria's fast-food service centers.

So we were at the seminar.

There were about 30 people in attendance at that seminar. It was a leadership seminar organized by Pat Utomi, a Nigerian professor of political economy, a management expert and a former presidential candidate. He made a fine spiel on entrepreneurship and leadership and supplied a stream of ideas.

I took some notes:

"If we want a better Nigeria, we need to create it. It will not just happen."

"We should not be tied to our past; we need to be tied to our potential."

"We will not grow unless we examine and reflect on our own life, get to know ourselves, and understand our own strengths, talents, and values. It's in developing these personal insights that provides the foundation for successful leadership."

Then I turned in my seat and watched Chidi nod his head. I couldn't help admiring his stunning good looks. I was proud of being his date. Every girl likes her guy cute. Or am I the only one?

The seminar didn't reach an official conclusion, but it was strongly leaning towards a utilitarian direction, and in effect, towards challenging us. I must say, the sessions offered the most interesting and practical insights I had ever heard – they were lightbulb moments where things just made sense. Suddenly, I had a way in which I could manage what I was doing effectively.

After the seminar, I thanked Chidi for taking me there.

I had no doubt that Chidi loved me and desired to see me grow as a brand. He was a big fan of AMAKAMEDIA. He even mostly preferred to call me "Amakamedia" and I didn't like that.

"Chidi, why do you call me Amakamedia?"
"Because that's you. You are Amakamedia."
"Chidi, don't call be Amakamedia. It's for the public. Call me something else when it's just the two of us."

Chidi, for some reasons, would rather see me as others saw me. But then again, I wanted him to have a very personal experience of me. I wanted to feel the delicacy in the uniqueness of what we share — love. I wanted to be the way he wanted me to be.

He preferred the public knowledge of me. Perhaps, he loved AMAKAMEDIA, not me.

He knew Amakamedia as a cheerful, creative, outgoing, career-oriented perfectionist who is always surrounded with people. He knew her as a woman who tried to look beautiful and self-confident and took a good care of herself. He knew her as a person who is able to help others. He was used to seeing me laughing and happy.

But I wanted him to see the real me. Shy. Broken. Lonely. Moody. Emotional.

Maybe he eventually did . . .and couldn't deal with it.

Maybe I was too intense for him.

His Jacket

We had to leave.

I shifted beside him and put my book away, yet he didn't move a muscle as if he wasn't aware I was there. He was lost in thought.

"What's on your mind?"
"Nothing."
"There is definitely something on your mind. Only a dead man has nothing on his mind. What's on your mind?"
"Nothing."

I pushed away from him, needing the distance. His cologne was messing with my head. I swallowed past the lump in my throat.

Right before we set out to leave, it started to rain.

Chidi took off his jacket and gave it to me to cover my hair so it wouldn't get wet. It was the sweetest thing.

We've all watched romantic movies where the guy gives his jacket to the girl he likes when it's cold out. It's something that happens in real life too. Chidi was the kind of guy who lends you his jacket to keep you warm even if he's cold. He would say he's fine, but he's probably not. It shows that he puts your needs first. He cares about you, and he doesn't want you to catch a cold.

Thinking about it again, Chidi was a nice guy. Just being nice.

Phone Sex

I remember how Chidi set my body on fire when he told me in a husky, excited tone that he wanted to pull my skirt off, unclasp my bra, and take my nipples between his lips. I remember the thrill of those blunt and brazen statements. The memory is enough to get my blood pumping even now.

Chidi and I never shared a bed, but we talked dirty over the phone. We shared what we were going to do if we eventually get married. We played with our imaginations. We fantasized.

"Baby, I'm going to touch you right there."
"Awww . . . I will bite you."
"I will gently stroke my hand around your neck."
"Oh! I will like that."

It wasn't a physical act but we felt it. We felt it strongly. I was wet. He had a "hard on". It was real.

We didn't start out to have phone sex that Wednesday night. He was even fasting during that period while I had just concluded mine. So you can imagine how spiritually minded we were. Indeed. We simply got talking and talking about everything and all.

We started to tease each other. And before we knew it, we were flirting!

In our slowest, most seductive and sultry tones, we created the scenario:

"Baby, what are you wearing?"
"I'm wearing a satin nightgown"
"Is it short?"
"Yea. Wait lemme guess you're wearing boxers."
"Yes. Can you guess what colour it is?"
"Blue?"
"No. Make another guess."
"Erm . . . is it brown?"
"No baby. It's striped in white, black and green."
"Oh. I almost mentioned black o."
"Hmm . . . How I wish I was there with you right now."
"Me too. What would you do with me if you were here?"

We went on and on.

I was caressing my breast and felt my nipple getting harder and harder. I was gently tracing my fingers right down to my panties and I could feel how wet I was down there.

It was the first time we had phone sex. My first time.

How We Broke Up

He just disappeared.
No word.

It is easy to see the beginning of a thing, but harder to see the end. I can remember with clarity like the stretch marks on my lower hip how Chidi and I met, but I cannot lay my finger on the moment it ended. The ambiguities, second starts and broken resolves cannot be cut through on a page to the point where he no longer existed.

With every day that passed, I felt him withdrawing. The connection between us was slipping further and further away. I found myself, shrinking into a corner, mimicking the distance I felt building between us. My moods were shifting all over the place.

Guys like Chidi are the ones who stop trying when it no longer feels like a challenge. They have won your heart and they don't see the need to keep trying to win you over again. They claim that love eventually fades away and there's nothing you can do about it.

Relationships ultimately die when you stop trying to be there for each other and when you stop doing all the little things that matter. They end when you stretch the gap between the two of you that you end up feeling like you are all alone – when you stop missing each other.

A relationship dies when you get too comfortable that you forget to show each other how much you care. It ends when you become so sure that they won't go anywhere so you stop showing appreciation or making an effort. When you start taking them for granted, when you stop thanking them for what they do, when you stop showing appreciation for who they are.

Relationships end when you kill love with your own hands.

Our relationship died. Just like that.

Lessons Learnt

1. <u>Acceptance</u>

I refused to succumb to the false belief that because this guy didn't want to be with me that I had no value or worth. I refused to surrender to the false hope that he would come back to me. Unlike my relationship with Ben, quite the opposite happened! I owned my value and supported myself in who I truly am. I rewired patterns. I grew out of a self-pity woeful post break-up girl to an empowered and proud self-valued woman.

It would be great to get an apology every time someone hurts us, but that's not reality. The reality is, sometimes, apologies don't come. But when we learn to accept our worth, we can also come to realize that we don't need someone else's apology in order to forgive and move on.

This self-acceptance was totally new for me and I started looking at myself with new eyes on a much deeper scale. The experience was difficult yet incredibly beautiful and transforming. My courage to rise in authenticity was liberating. I still hold respect for Chidi and I hold respect for myself. I am constantly leaning into the lessons that I am freaking awesome, life does in fact *go on* and I am totally fine.

Acceptance is believing that we want to know the truth, and there is a part of us, our heart that recognizes the truth. When we cling to the truth, we become aware of the motivation behind our choices and then, we are liberated to live in freedom.

2. <u>Some Relationships Simply Come to Teach Us How to Gracefully Let Go</u>

I had to stop looking for answers. I had to stop asking why the relationship ended and move on.

Letting go gracefully, with complete forgiveness and love for the other person requires understanding and self-forgiveness. Being able to let go of the past allowed me to be fully present emotionally, spiritually and physically in future relationships.

I realized love is not something to be rushed. It is something to be valued when you share the same feeling.

When you love someone, there is a possibility the feeling might not be mutual. It's best to not invest in a feeling that only you can feel. It's best to not let any guy treat you like a choice, because girl, you deserve more than being an option.

I'm better off alone, enjoying every little thing around me than spending my time trying to be someone's one and only, when all he's trying to prove is that I'm just his pastime. I deserve to feel like I'm important, because a real man sees the real worth of a girl and makes her his number one priority.

Girl, it's not that you're not good enough for him, it's that he's not good enough for you. Don't ever settle for less.

I was first consumed by the idea that I lost the man who I see my future with, the man I imagine to be with me through ups and downs. But then I realized, it wasn't my loss. It was his.

3. Sexual Purity Is Vital

Chidi and I never really discussed boundaries. . .I mean, why would we? He was a Christian. I was a Christian. No worries there, right?

It's true that Chidi and I never had sex. But we played it over again in our minds. It took grace for us to not do it. We seriously prayed to stay chaste before marriage. We thought having phone sex was safe. That was a lie! Phone sex will do more harm than good in any beautiful relationship that is heading towards a kingdom marriage.

I have come to understand and believe that having phone sex is NOT a good thing for those who are keen on walking into godly relationships . . .

- Because phone sex is based on your imagination, you and your partner will be setting each other up for unreasonable expectations. Reality doesn't always match imagination; you know?

- You are preparing yourselves for giving in to temptation. There are going to be times when you both are alone and the temptation for sex before marriage will be harder to resist because your conversations have been sexual.

- It will become so easy to slip into sexual conversations. Sex is not all there is in marriage. You should be spending time getting to know each other while courting - personality, character and values. Not to fulfill sexual desires.

I think when many people today discuss sexual purity, they confuse *purity* with *virginity*. They place value on whether or not one is a virgin, not if they have compromised any other part of their body or mind to maintain their virginity.

The quest for purity is beyond avoiding fornication (or adultery). As a matter of fact, to be *pure* means to be chaste, holy, innocent, not contaminated. It has more to do with sexual propriety - AVOIDING any form of immorality in thought, word, and action.

There is much more to living purely than abstaining from sexual intercourse. Purity is a lifestyle. It is an everyday mode of being. Purity is not a choice. It is an instruction from God.

You can't claim to be pure even as a virgin when you derive sexual pleasure from pressing, licking, sucking, kissing, holding, etc. Of course, it feels good. It is natural for a girl and a guy to want to further explore the nakedness of each other. It is natural to be stimulated or aroused by the sights, sounds, touch, or even smells of each other. It is so hard to live purely, because it is a constant fight against our flesh, over what is natural. However, we have to remember that purity is a sacred gift from God.

4. Forgiving Is Not Forgetting

If you want to forget someone you love, I'm sorry you will never fully forget. Your heart might stop yearning and your dreams will no longer haunt. One day, you might even be convinced you are done with missing and your wounds are healed. But deep down, you will know you can only wish it was true because if you see the person, if you have a chance, just a chance to love them like you've always wanted, you still cannot be sure you would give it up.

You will never forget someone you love and the love that's borne out of sincerity and moments of truths. The good news is, you will learn to clean up your thoughts and ease up your feelings. Then over time, you will start to believe your own truths.

I have forgiven Chidi but I will never forget him because the truth is, a part of me has never really wanted to. I don't want to forget all the times we spent together, all the ways he made me feel, the laughter and tears, the pain and happiness. I want to carry it all with me no matter how deep it hurts because it's what makes me and this life worth living.

Nwamaka Onyekachi
@Amakamedia

Forget it, Nigerian guys are cute. Especially the dark ones.

9:48 PM - 14 Dec 2014 from Ikeja, Nigeria

CHAPTER SIX

Jerry

"Being deeply loved by someone gives you strength while loving someone deeply gives you courage." - Tao Tzu

Oh, Jerry. I never doubted you. Our love story started in a very promising way and felt like a fairy tale. I honestly thought you were the one. I told the world about you. I told everyone how we met and how we were going to end up being married. Is it really true that our relationship didn't lead to marriage? I never would have thought.

Our relationship was a brief one but it made a major impact in my heart. It went deep.

I really can't start typing afresh how we met and how much we shared. I will have to go back to my blog and copy the things I had written about you. About us. The Magic I found in you and The Wonder that you saw in me. Everything you ever meant to me. . .

How We Met

It was a Sunday. I had just had the most amazing evening house fellowship meeting ever. And I was smiling my way back home as I hummed a song, *Imeela. . .Imeela. . .okaka. . .onye kere uwa. . .imeela. . .imeela. . .Eze'm oo. . .*

I was such in a good mood. Perhaps in high spirits. I didn't realize I had a smile on my face until he smiled back at me. *Huh?* I waved and kept on walking.

He ran after me.

"Hi!" he greeted as he approached me.

"Hey!" I replied, still smiling.

"I've seen you somewhere before."

"Really? Oh I see." Although I've heard many guys say those familiar words, yet I stopped to hear him out.

He was wearing a black shirt on blue jeans. He looked very masculine. He had glasses but took them off. I didn't look at his feet, so I can't tell whether he was barefoot or not.

He said, "I'm not like them. I am a very reasonable person. I don't just see a girl on the street and run after her. My time is money. I'm talking to you for a reason."

I think he had an accent but his cuteness covered up for it. *Or maybe I'm only assuming.*

He continued, "I know what you're thinking. You think I want to collect your number and call you up, and then sleep with you."

I can't remember what I said next. But it sounded like, "Ahh!"

"No. Far from it. I'm a very reasonable person. I control my urges. I worked with models. I can stay in a room full of naked girls and not be moved."

But why is this guy telling me all these na? I pinched myself for wasting my time giving him the time.

"Ok, I'm sorry. I have to go now. . ." I muttered as I showed him the Bible I was holding. "As you can see, I went for house fellowship and..."

"What is it? Why are you being stiff? Loosen up!" he blurted.

I laughed. And I hated that I laughed because my laughter made him laugh too. So we had a laughter moment which felt rather awkward.

"You can't be with Jerry and not laugh," he bragged.

"D-u-h!" I smirked

"So what's your name?" he asked as he looked at my eyes. Looked down to my nose. Then to my lips.

"My name is Amaka," I coyly responded.

"That's good." He nodded.

I don't know how he did it but we got talking for almost an hour. His phone rang about three times, but he rejected the calls as we were lost in the conversation. And Jerry never stopped saying, "I am a very reasonable person."

So we did exchange phone numbers after all. And I saved his name as *Jerreasonable*.

I got home and thought, *I should blog about this.*

Memorable Moments
<u>The Phone Calls</u>

*12 missed calls. . .*and Jerry was still calling. I had refused to pick up his calls because I thought I might fall in love with him. I had a high tendency of falling in love easily as well as falling out of love quickly. No, I wasn't a love junkie. No.

These are days when you can easily reach your loved ones via social media platforms such as BBM, Facebook, Twitter, WhatsApp and the likes. These platforms make communication easier, faster and cheaper. Unfortunately, Jerry only had my phone number. So he depended solely on phone calls.

Jerry: Hello dear
Amaka: Hey you
Jerry: How are you dear?
Amaka: I'm fine ooo
Jerry: Have you eaten?
Amaka: Yea
Jerry: What did you eat?
Amaka: Erm. . . bread and fish-stew
Jerry: That's okay. What are you doing now?
Amaka: Doing studio things. Trying to edit a jingle. What about you?
Jerry: Work. Work. Work. We are working on our launch project. It's been all work for me *sighs*
Amaka: Eeyah. . . but the koko is that you enjoy what you do na.
Jerry: True. I'm not complaining. All we need is God's grace. This is my purpose. My destiny. My life. I can't joke with it.
Amaka: Hmmmm. . .

I liked that Jerry was purpose-driven.

He always talked about fulfilling his purpose and living a life with meaning. Hearing him say those words got me tripping.

Jerry had become my first caller every morning and last caller every night. We talked about our day and whatever we were working on.

~phone rings again~
It's Jerreasonable.

I still wouldn't pick up. This guy should leave me alone biko. I shrugged.

~phone beeps~
Jerry sent me an SMS.

Amaka plz cn u pikup & tel me
wts goin on?

I dnt reali undrstnd.... Wts
hapening? I dnt gt like seriously,
dis new developmnt... Plz pikup
& explain

"Amaka, please can you pick up and tell me what's going on?"

Magic and Wonder

"Did anybody call you?" Bro. Ignatius asked me.

"Somebody like who?"

"One man came here on Tuesday to collect your number. I think he needs you to create a jingle for him because he mentioned it. So I gave it to him."

Bro. Ignatius attended Bible study that week but I didn't. So it was during Sunday service that he told me about some man who came looking for me, asking for my number.

Who could it be? I had no idea who he might be.

I had started picking Jerry's calls again because he just wouldn't give up. *Was I that awesome and fun to be with?* His persistence made an impression on me.

So Jerry and I fixed a meeting. Actually, it was a date. Our first date.

We went to an eatery not very far from home. We talked, laughed and made jest of each other. He told me how much he cared and how he felt helpless about his feelings. He painfully tried to explain how he couldn't find the reasons behind his desire to have me in his life.

I wanted to tell him that the feeling was mutual but I didn't. I had my fears too. He told me he went to my church hoping to find me there. He had really wanted to see me and to understand why I hadn't been picking up his calls.

Oh! He was the one Bro. Ignatius talked about.

"When you don't pick my calls, it hurts me. I've never been this patient with anyone before. When I want something from somebody, and I don't get it almost immediately, I lose interest completely. But with you. . ." He paused.

We kissed.

It just happened. And it felt like magic when we first kissed. I wanted more. I was such a *good bad girl.*

We kissed again.

"Baby, you're a wonder," he said as he looked into my eyes while holding my chin.

"You. . . are. . . magic," I whispered.

We sat there wondering about what we had done and what we were going to do next. *Or perhaps I was the only one thinking I had committed a sin by kissing!*

He held out my hands, looked into my eyes and spoke in the calmest voice ever. He told me he needed me to be his soul-mate. To help his ministry. To walk with him on the journey to fulfilling purpose. Jerry made the commitment to love and cherish my heart.

So, there I was giving love a chance. He called me "Wonder" and I called him "Magic".

<u>Jerry Knows Somehow</u>

I still hadn't gotten over our first kiss. The memory was still fresh. It must have been a magic kissing spell or something, because it never left my mind ever since. The butterflies were already building a mansion in my stomach. *Will they ever leave*? I wondered.

I could imagine God laughing at me that morning as I prayed about my feelings. Anyone who heard me praying might have had a laugh attack. It was so funny that I found it funny too:

Dear Lord, please help me put those kisses into perspective. We got so carried away with our emotions. It was nothing really. I'm sorry I responded. I shouldn't have but it was so. . . no I mean, forgive me. It's so hard to say no to Jerry. I don't know how to resist his kisses anymore. I feel so helpless now. Please, help me get pass these. . .growing feelings I have for him. I think I love him. Oh Lord, I don't really understand. . .please help me. . .just help me. . .help me to do Your will.

I can't deny it. I really liked being around Jerry, and I loved the way he treated me. He gave me all his love and attention. And I was like "Am I dreaming?!"

I melted in his muscular arms. I blushed at his gazes. My heart raced at how he expressed his love. Time stood still when we talked and shared moments together.

It felt so right to be with Jerry, but then again it was scary. Maybe because it was all happening so fast. I was not sure whether it was a good thing to be afraid to love and be loved. Blessedly, I had asked God to help me in that situation. *Or what do I call it?*

Love.

And Just when I thought the story had ended. Jerry made me realize the story had only just begun.

Focus

"Are you never going to kiss me again?" I asked Jerry. We'd already had two different dates after our first kiss. And still, he wouldn't kiss me. Why?

We had a dinner date. A date we had both looked forward to. The last time I'd seen him was about 24 hours ago but it'd felt like 24 years. *How I missed my Magic!*

I was in a long flowery dress and he was smartly dressed in jeans. We talked, laughed and enjoyed some silence. Being with Jerry was like breathing - he gave me life.

A part of me was craving for his kisses. The other part of me was loving him for every second he didn't kiss me. The good girl in me sure wanted to be good but the bad girl in me just wouldn't shut her trap.

"Are you saying you're never going to kiss me again?"

"Baby, I love you," he said calmly.

"Can you just answer my question, please?!" I snapped.

"I love you scatter," he demonstrated the *scatter* with his hands, and smiled.

Does this man think I'm joking? I didn't smile back at him. Instead, I put up a straight face.

"Baby, I need you to understand something. . ."

I cut in, "It's either a yes or a no."

"You need to understand something." He had that serious look on his face which always kept me in check. Always.

"What is it?" Suddenly, I was interested.

"I need you to know that I love you."

"Ugh!" I was pissed.

Who is talking about love here?! I'm talking about kiss, Mister Man. Jerry. . .kiss me! I screamed on the inside.

As he observed my disposition, he said, "Come here."

We were sitting very close; I mean very close. His lips could reach my lips from there. But he still wanted me to come.

Whenever Jerry said "Come here" even when I was just right beside him, he wanted me to lean on him so he could wrap his muscular arms around me. Something told me he knew just how magical I felt in his welcoming arms. Well, I always ran into those arms - the arms of the one who was holding my heart.

"Wonder, I love you so much and I respect your body. I can't touch you because I love God. I love my purpose. And I love you," he said as he stroked my hair.

I sat up immediately. "Wait o! Like no more kissing. Is that it?"

"Baby, you are safe. You will be fine. I need us to have a pure and godly relationship."

The thoughts in my head were in a sprint race. I couldn't think for a minute. I was numb. Then I closed my eyes. "But why did you kiss me the first time?" I asked with my eyes still closed.

"Erm. . .you know. . . it was an emotional moment for us. So. . . we got into the mood. . . and we kissed," he replied gently.

"Baby, I'm sorry," he added.

"You shouldn't have kissed me the first time!" I pushed back the tears that had tried to fall. "You started it. You sparked me up. And now you are telling me we are never going to ki. . ."

He grabbed me. "Oh baby, I'm sorry. I didn't mean to hurt you. It is hard for me too. It's a tough decision to make. Why can I not kiss and have sex with the woman I truly love? It is because I love God and I love you. I want us to have the best marriage ever. Can we make it work?"

This is the man I dreamed. The man who is determined to let the marriage bed pure and undefiled. The man who loves and obeys God. The man who loves and respects my body. How can I not love him?!

I looked up to heaven and breathed, "Thank You, Lord."

Lord, help us stay focused. Especially me!

<u>Goodbye Jerreasonable</u>

It would make more sense if Jerry and I were taking a walk on the beach right now. I thought to myself.

We took a walk down the street. And I did not exactly enjoy walking with Jerry on a busy road. The noise on the streets which included cars hooting, people shouting and all that, distracted me from savouring the moment.

"So did you miss me?" Jerry asked.

I was walking right next him, but I was lost in my own thoughts. I couldn't remember what I was thinking about, maybe it was something the two girls who were walking behind us had mentioned. For a moment, it appeared like I snubbed him.

"I see you don't like walking and talking," he said.

I sensed a bit of anger in his tone. "Oh, I'm sorry. I'm just not in the mood," I lied.

"I know you. I get it. You'd prefer we sit down to face each other while we talk."

"Hmm. . ." *I thought so too.* "I'm sorry," I quickly apologized.

"It's okay."

"I love you my baby boo," I said, with a sound of laughter in my voice.

"I don't really like that name. Don't call me that dear."

"*Ahan,* so what should I now call you?"

"Whatever you like but not that name used in all those ungodly relationships. We are not like them. We are different. "

You are right. I don't like it too. That was the first and last time I ever called him *Baby boo.*

Jerry loved it when I addressed him with sincere, warm, and lovely names. Now, these were the names I called him - My magic. My heart. My love. My hero. My king.

Yeah. I also liked it when he did same to me. I blushed when he said I am -
His wonder. His baby. His love. His world. His queen.

Each of these names meant a lot to our relationship. Jerry and I were as
real as we could ever be. Everything happened so naturally.

Jerreasonable no longer existed. He was gone. But I still had "My Magic".

<u>Chats of Solomon</u>

Then we chatted on social media because the phone calls weren't just
enough. I really did enjoy the dynamics of social media and the power of
emoticons.

If Jerry and I were in a competition of "Who is more romantic?", it would
be a tie. We were too romantic at almost the same level. Being romantic is
saying or doing things that show that you love someone. And Jerry and I
expressed our feelings for each other without any doubt or shame. We did
not care who texted first, or replied last.

We couldn't help to say, "I love you."

When we didn't talk about our love, we felt like we were lying to each
other. We did not pretend. We did not hide it. We were in love!

The other night, we were chatting on one of the social media platforms.
Like. . .

Jerry: Where is my baby???
Amaka: She is right here :)

Jerry: Ah I missed you ooo
Amaka: I missed you too
Jerry: My baby
Amaka: My love
Jerry: My wonder
Amaka: My magic
Jerry: Baby, you are awesome
Amaka: You are amazing
Jerry: You are precious
Amaka: You are adorable
Jerry: You are positively weird
Amaka: Weird? Eewo! You are strange
Jerry: Lol. You are a dream come true
Amaka: You are mine!
Jerry: You be my own
Amaka: Carry go! Lmho
Jerry: Baby, sincerely, you are the true definition of love. I love you
Amaka: I love you too

As I went through our chat the next morning, I had a glimpse of the Book of Songs of Solomon.

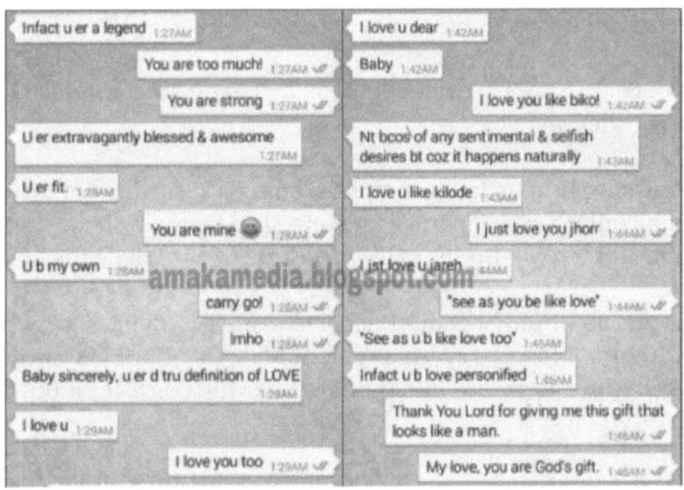

Then I said to myself, *Mehn! this can pass for the Book of Chats of Solomon!*

<u>**Another Her**</u>

Jerry's line had been off all morning. I was worried-sick. "*What is happening??*"

Each time my phone rang, I had just one person on my mind. Just one.

I had received quite a number of calls that morning. But none of them was Jerry's. I was disappointed when each voice I heard was not his.

For the umpteenth time, I dialed his number again. Still, I couldn't get through to him.

I was neither angry nor sad. In fact, I was more afraid than worried. I kept talking to myself.

"What is happening?"
"Well, maybe he is very busy and does not want to be disturbed."
"Oh, am I now a distraction?"
"Wait. He must have misplaced his phone. Who knows?"
"What if he's not feeling well?"
"Oh God, please can I just know he is ok?"
"I miss him. I miss him. I miss him."
"I know I can be very annoying sometimes. Maybe he is even angry with me."
"Has he stopped loving me?"
"Jerry, please call me. . . now. . . please!"

Five minutes gone. . .twenty minutes gone. . .an hour gone. . .three hours gone. . .Jerry hasn't called me yet.

"I'm here missing him. Is he even missing me?" I hissed as I muttered to myself. I was falling sick. Then I agreed to stop trying to reach him. I made up my mind not to pick up his calls even if he eventually calls me back.

But how long can I hold? I cannot deceive myself. I love Jerry too much not worry about him. I love Jerry too much not to care about his lines being switched off. I love Jerry too much not to hear his voice right now.

Again I dialed his number. *Phew!* How I hated that lady who kept saying, "Sorry, the number you have dialed is switched off."

She is so evil. If I catch her. . .

Event Wear

It was 8:45 PM. I still couldn't get through to Jerry. This might probably be the first day he never called since the day we met. But I hoped not.

I had completed all the items I had on my to-do list. It wasn't a very bad day. But Jerry could have made it much better if he had called. He didn't. Perhaps not yet.

As I lay on the bed alone with my pillows, I thought about Jerry. I thought about the happy moments we shared. I thought about the way he made me blush. I thought about the day we. . .

. . . That day we were at an eatery. It wasn't the same eatery where we had our first kiss. We had a good time there anyway. While we were talking, I showed him a picture on my phone which I had thought he'd like. Alas, he didn't hide his feelings. He hated the dress.

"Why will you expose your boobs like this na? It is called private part. A private part should not be seen in public."

"Erm. . .but it's not exactly exposed o. Besides, it was a bridal dress. And it is very expensive."

"So? It is expensive. And so? How much is worth your dignity as a woman? Don't wear this dress again biko."

"Ah! Me I like it and I . . . "

He cuts in. "Baby, you should represent purity in your fashion. I need you to..."

I dozed off.

Few minutes later, my phone started ringing. At first, I heard it in my sleep until it sounded loud enough to wake me up. Unfortunately, the phone stopped ringing before I finally opened my eyes. So I missed the call.

"Oh my God! It's Magic!" I gasped.

I found 9 Missed calls and 3 text messages. They were all from Jerry. He had been calling since 9:12 PM.

I read the first and second text messages. He said he was sorry. Then the third. . .

Wait a minute! He didn't just address me by my first name, but he also spelt it wrongly. "What?!"

Small Shakara

When a man loves a woman, he tells her. When a woman loves a man, she tells the world. I had just added another personal love quote to my diary. I smiled.

It dawned on me. Love is a beautiful thing but it can also be painful. You have to fight to keep it. You have to nurture it to grow. And you have to get angry to appreciate it. Yeah, I think so.

I was angry.

I was angry with myself for letting this man who came from nowhere sweep me off my feet. I was angry with myself for allowing this man to make me fall helplessly in love with him. I was angry with myself for thinking about this man at every second of the day. I was angry with myself for being angry with this man.

I hadn't spoken to Jerry since I read that text message in which he wrongly spelt my name. I had refused to pick up his calls or reply his messages. *I think I needed a deliverance from the spirit of malice.*

Deep down in my heart, I wanted to hear his voice. I had missed him. But I was still not picking up his calls. *Why was I like that?*

I wanted him to know I wasn't happy with him. He already knew I wasn't in a good mood. But he didn't know he was in trouble with me.

Phone rings.
Phone rings. "Don't you think this man has tried enough?" I ignored it.
Phone rings. I shrugged.
Phone rings.

After a while, I picked up his call. It might not have been the sweetest phone call in the world, but it was one of the truest calls my heart has ever received.

~Excerpts from the call~

Amaka: . . .and then you misspelt my name.
Jerry: Oh my Wonder, I'm sorry. It was a typo. No vex.
Amaka: Hmm. . . oya spell my name correctly now.
Jerry: *Laughs* Ok ma, N-W-A-M-A-K-A. I love you anyhow.
Amaka: *Giggles* I love you too.

Sometimes, Jerry and I seemed like a perfect match made from heaven. Other times I wondered what a mess we were together. But most times, I felt my heart was so naked that he could see right through it. He knew the exact words my heart wanted him to say. *How much more magical can he be?*

> U av touched my heart & filled my
> world wit so much love...
> WONDER I love U more & more wit
> each passing day. Comot 4 hier
> jhorr, which kind love b dis self???

Jerry loved me very much. That was why I could do small shakara.

How It Ended

Jerry stopped calling me as regularly as he used to.
Jerry wouldn't reply my chats until several days after.
He promised to change but he never did.

The last time we spoke about this issue, he was like:
"Baby, I'm sorry. I've been too busy lately. You're always on my mind.
Always. When I don't call you, you should know I'm thinking of you."
In my mind, I was like: *"Really? Was he not busy before I met him?"*

I grew tired of his excuses of being busy all the time. I gave him many
chances and was patient with him, but I was pained for what he was
doing. *Avoiding me. . . and killing me!*

One random day, not random I must say, he sent me a text message.

Hi dear,hw u doin? Gues u'er
owk! Jst wanna apologise 4 evry
emotional troma av put u tru...
Lukin @ tins d way dey'er nw,i
cnt gve u d attention u deserve
nw & wil nt wnt dt 2 continue & 2
put u tru anymore emotional
pain! I luv u enuf nt 2 put u in
pains nevr again, Dats y i wanna
kal it off.. Ef its indeed God's wil
we b 2geda, it wil b bt 4 nw! Lets
jst b frnds... Am sori 4 evrytin
indeed.

"Let's just be friends?" The rug on which I was standing was pulled from underneath my feet. In fact, my feet could no longer carry me. I could not understand what was happening and why so sudden. I thought we were happy . . .I thought I was being a great girlfriend. . .I thought we were going in a good direction. I thought he was my husband.

I was devastated, I was confused, and I was completely lost without him. I was hurt, so deeply hurt, and there was no way seeing it through; it was unbearable. I put my identity into that relationship. It was so glorious in my eyes, so fun, so fascinating, so vibrant, and so magical. I was infatuated with him and everything about him: his eyes, his body, his laugh . . .I was in complete awe of him.

When I lost him, I lost it all. I was on a very high cloud and the fall was nothing near exhilarating or pleasant. I cried myself to sleep countless nights. I prayed to God to bring him back to me, but He didn't. I stopped wishing Jerry would come back, then I found love in my sewing machine. My love for sewing with Ankara fabric was birthed.

Lessons Learnt

1. Becoming More Self-Aware

Although it was excruciating, the greatest and most powerful offering I learned from that heartbreak was discovering myself - my true self.

I began questioning myself, my views, and my outlooks on life. I started connecting with the world around me. I took a deep dive into the matters of my heart and God's word lifted me out of my slump. In retrospect, I am grateful to God for that breakup. I am grateful I experienced the ultimate depths of despair because it catapulted me onto the path of Self: Self-realization, Self-discovery, and Self-love. It took me some time, but I did eventually forgive him. I forgave him first energetically through journaling; then years later on I *thanked* him for launching me onto this path!

I discovered I was the toxic one.

Jerry made me know how much of a blither I was — crazy and would throw a fight every time I didn't get what I wanted. I would call and deliberately say the most painful things just so he could be sorry. I was overly jealous and a control freak, and gave Jerry grief for things he did which I thought betrayed me, even though they weren't truly the case.

A failed relationship isn't always about what the guy did wrong or how he wasn't right for you. Sometimes you're the one that ruins a good thing. Thankfully, you can learn from those mistakes and become a better person, and a better potential spouse, in the process.

To marry, to merge, to become one, to unify with another person is a process of full exposure. If you don't work on knowing yourself, working on your flaws and improving your capacity now, then you will most likely be heading towards a frustrating future with another guy.

The greatest thing about each relationship we have is it serves as mirror for where we need to grow. In Part 3 of this book, you will see how God turned me inside-out when I let Him.

2. Knowing God Is Knowing Love

Being in love with someone doesn't mean you have to spend every waking hour with the person, merge your identity with theirs, and forget about your own dreams. Finding love means making the most of the moments you have together while also honouring God. The time you spend apart should have you doing the things that make you feel alive.

In some twisted way, I thought I was loving Jerry right, but I was worshipping him. He was the first and last thing on my mind. I made him a god. I honoured him more than I honoured God. At the time, my relationship with God wasn't a priority. I wasn't putting God second (or third or fifth for that matter).

It's terrible to lose yourself in the process of loving another. Get to know yourself. Get to know God. Spend time with yourself. Spend time with God.

A relationship will only work if you have discovered God's true love for you and love yourself as well as the guy the way God intends all His children to be loved.
You cannot understand your identity, purpose or accept who and what you are without understanding who God is, your creator and source of all things.

Identity: The condition of being one's self
Purpose: The reason for which something exists
Acceptance: The act of assenting or believing (believing who you are)

These three areas of understanding come through a relationship and the knowledge of yourself in Christ.

YOUR purpose, YOUR identity, acceptance and love for all that is YOUR being must be acquired in singleness, internally in Christ.

You must understand these things about your individual self before you can even identify a guy and put your relationship with him into the right perspective.

Heartbreak, pain and disappointment will always manifest if you do not have deep internal knowledge of God. You have to know yourself, your purpose and accept yourself as defined by the word of God.

3. Letting Go Is Letting God

Letting go of the life I thought I'd live was the hardest thing I've ever done. Letting go of the idea of Jerry was gut-wrenching. One thing I have come to understand is that people come together for each person's maximum spiritual, emotional and mental growth. And when the growth is done, it's time for an end. Even if they left without saying goodbye, guess what? It's all good! It's time to move on. LET IT GO. The relationship didn't work out because it just wasn't meant to be or the timing was over.

Psychologists say much like when someone close to you dies, losing a relationship will take you through the five stages of grief:

I. Denial
ii. Anger
iii. Bargaining
iv. Depression and
v. Acceptance.

I went through each stage over and over again before getting to acceptance.
I kept on telling myself:

Don't deny it. Let it go.
Release the images and emotions. . .
Release the grudges and fears. . .
Release the clinging and disappointments of the past. . .
Let go, let God.
Let go, let God.
If you don't let it go, you'll be stuck.
Don't be afraid to let go
You are enough.
Trust God to bring the people you need.
Embrace new friendships.
Don't deny it. Let Go.

The beautiful thing is when I let go, I let God.

Nwamaka Onyekachi
@Amakamedia

I thought I could be holy by simply being a "good girl", I was shocked how I easily fell.

Only the grace of God can make us holy.

5:59 AM · 17 May 17 · Twitter for Android

CHAPTER SEVEN

Enitan

"Love believes all things. Love hopes all things. Love endures all things."
- I Corinthians 13:7, ESV

Technically, you never asked but I knew you would ask me to marry you one day. I knew that ring — maybe stupidly big or maybe modest and subtle — was constantly at the back of your mind. I heard you talking to friends, sisters and your parents about it. About me. About us.

So even though the words "will you marry me?" never actually came out of your mouth I knew they lingered at the back of your mind, waiting for the perfect time, the perfect place, the perfect moment. You waited for what you thought would seem as the "perfect" moment for me, maybe because you knew I cherish moments a lot.

I felt like a walking cliché every time your name came up. I felt like a fraud, like a fabrication of the person you used to kiss on the forehead and say "I love you" to when you thought I enjoyed the meat pie you bought. But even though I hate myself a little every time I lament how difficult it was, I was telling the truth.

Leaving you was one of the hardest decisions I have ever made.

A life with you was the smart choice. Staying with you and your level-headedness and your ability to always be reasonable would have been a good match for a somewhat overly emotional person like me. You gave my existence a balance.

I missed that for quite a while.

I could see our future, with the lack of pain because of your peaceful nature and the stretch marks on my stomach from giving you the children you were so certain you would love, but I wasn't sure about what I wanted. You tried to paint a picture of us in five years, and I could see that it was almost like those versions of us already existed and were right there with you. You tried to convince me that you were the right choice. And I wanted to want you, I really did. I wanted to enjoy talking about baby names, who would be at our wedding party and where we would live.

But I didn't.

At 19, I wasn't built for the relationship that you were trying to claw out of me. I had many mistakes to make and experiences to have that didn't involve a totally committed relationship. I needed to be selfish. And obviously, I couldn't do that with you there to hold my hand. I just wanted to find myself. Be myself. All by myself.

You said you would miss me when you left me there at the table, crying because I knew I was setting myself free at your own expense. I think about you and wonder if you do. I know you're in love again and that makes me happy. Slightly jealous too, if we are being transparent here. But I'm happy for you because I want you to have everything you've always wanted.

Well, I wish you think of me. Do you?

I hope you think of me for even a split second, from time to time.

I'm sorry. I'm so sorry I couldn't be that person you needed me to be when we were still together. I'm sorry the thought of you wanting to get down on one knee didn't make me want to stay. I'm sorry I didn't want to walk down the aisle with you.

I'm sorry I broke your heart.

I saw a photo of you on social media. You were smiling with someone else and there was no longing to touch the beards I used to know so well. It's more of a twinge from not knowing where you are, what you are up to and not hearing your voice in years. Oh my. . .has it really been nine years?

I hope you are indeed happy.
I hope you are well.
I hope you are at peace.
Most of all, I hope you are given the love you deserve.
Once again, I'm sorry I couldn't marry you, but I believe by choosing not to we're both in better places.
At least, I hope so.

How We Met

Enitan met me at secondary school, but I met him after I graduated from secondary school. At least, that was when he confessed his identity as my secret admirer for three years. He sure deserves some accolades.

Memorable Moments

<u>Write For You</u>

Enitan's level-headedness, admiration, compassion, and love, was not lost on me. That Saturday, as I did my house chores, the lines just popped out — one by one — and soon, I sat down to write the whole poem, afraid I might lose one thought.

I can't remember the exact words I chose but it was a poem about us — our story — attending the same school, having the same teachers, knowing the same people, and living in the same city. It tied us into a harmony; an identical history leading to an identical future. It gave us hope for a future together.

I saw him later that evening and handed him the poem.

He was, to say, quite astonished. He read it aloud. He couldn't hide his delight at the words. He promised to keep the paper for as long as he could. He told me he was going to show me at our wedding anniversary.

He was the first guy to tell me I am a good writer.

<u>Indirectly Better</u>

Guys like Enitan will adore you. He would look at you when you are not looking, and when you look at him he would look away. He doesn't want you to think he's a creep when you constantly catch him looking at you, so he looks away quickly. Unfortunately, he's not quick enough sometimes. Anyways, when he looks at you, he's trying to build up the courage to talk to you. He thinks about approaching you, but then he backs down. It happens for a couple more times. It could be his lack of confidence. He fears he might make a fool of himself.

 "Can I ask you a hypothetical question?"
"Sure."
"Promise me you'll answer it."
"I promise."
"Promise me you'll not say no."

"Ahh. . ."
"Actually, it's not a yes or no question. I just don't want you to use style to avoid answering me. Promise?"
"OK *o*. I've heard."
He asked, "What would you say if I asked you to be my date for my friend's wedding?"

He could not ask me to be his date directly. He wanted to know the answer before he could formally ask me the question, in case I was going to say no. Apparently, rejection would be less painful with hypothetical questions.

"Well, when is the wedding?" I asked.
"Next month."
"Oh, there is a real wedding?"

He bit his bottom lip.

I caught him. He knew I knew he liked me so much to want me to marry him. He had been planning our future together, both in his head and now out in the open. Enitan liked me. He loved me. He adored me. He respected me.

He stood up and went into his room.
He came out with a book, "I got this for you."

I collected the book. Looked at it. I read the title -The Power of a Praying Woman.

"I don't know why but I am jealous. I am jealous of the man you would marry if it is not me."

I was stupefied.

I began to thaw, my bewilderment subverted by wonder. My view of him shifted.

I am going to be A Praying Woman.

"Thank you, Enitan."

<u>Meet My Sister</u>

Enitan wanted me to meet all the members of his family.So I met his mum, dad, cousins, uncle, aunty, and sister.

They loved me.

I was so sure they believed I was going to end up marrying Enitan.

He talked about me to everybody.

Damn! I didn't hear what they said! Were they talking about me?

I slid into an autopilot mode of self-preservation anytime he introduced me to people and I suppose I performed well enough, spoke at appropriate moments and smiled when necessary but I wasn't really paying attention.

He said we would move to Lagos Island together, our fingers entwined, looking at apartments and talking about how lovely it would be to have one of them to ourselves. It sounds ridiculous, but it certainly didn't feel like it at the time. I guess that was love, right?

How It Ended

I never thought it would hurt.

It took everything in me to finally realize that it's totally normal. Sometimes, the right decision is the most difficult. I couldn't fix my feelings. I already fixed what I could simply by ending a broken relationship. It was the best for both of us, even if it didn't feel like it then.

At lunch, I told him "Enitan, I'm not the right woman for you."
His face quickly went from concern to confusion.
I had to do it.

I did because I had finally realized that we had both assumed each other to be somewhat ideal mates which we were definitely not.

I did because I had accepted the fact that we were only dragging each other apart from our career-based priorities and not exactly complementing each other's growth.

I did because I did not see any future ahead for us anymore. Probably, also because I did not want to see any future.

I did because it was the only wise thing to do. For both of us.

I did because we needed some peace of mind and that was only possible with us parting ways.

All I could do was wish the best for the two of us.

Lesson Learnt

I found myself thinking about this old boyfriend — a person who I hadn't thought about in years. I realized that, although we weren't meant to be for many reasons, his presence in my life had been a positive influence. At such a young age, he taught me how men can be good and what a healthy relationship can look like. It was then — more than a decade later — that I realized, my time spent with him wasn't a waste, but a gift.

Maybe I needed that isolation and loneliness to evaluate exactly where I wanted to go from there without any distractions. Maybe I needed a lesson in putting myself first for once. Maybe I needed to lose love to realize there were still parts of me that needed to learn how to love myself and that couldn't be found in even the best relationship.

Maybe I needed a heartbreaking goodbye to finally take steps towards where and who I needed to be. Maybe I needed to find a relationship only to lose it to learn gratitude and appreciation for someone so good and kind. Maybe I needed to learn to let go.

Maybe I needed to fall apart so I could learn to put myself back together again. Maybe I needed to learn that an ending I might not like didn't mean the story wasn't a good one.

Maybe God was preparing me for something. Maybe.

CHAPTER EIGHT

Farouq

"Let all that you do be done in love." - 1 Corinthians 16:14, ESV

Everybody had a boyfriend except me.

I had no guy in the picture. I wanted a guy to call my own by all means. And there you were.

I liked how indifferent and "cool" you seemed, but I didn't really plan on hooking up with you. I was excited about this new free life, and opened to meeting new friends. I just wanted to say YES to any fun opportunity. It was my season of hoe-ishness. I kid.

I was not necessarily attracted to you. I made it quite clear that I just wanted to be your girlfriend for the time being. I told you specifically not to fall in love with me (which I now know is a guarantee someone will fall in love with you). But this just made you want me more. Flowers, poems, gifts, promises, compliments, home-cooked meals, intelligent-seeming conversation, great kiss. And my first Blackberry. You gave me everything.

Your appearance and style pretty much looked the same as they did, but for the first time, I started noticing your personality. You were funny - as in super funny. You had a great sense of humour, and you could make me laugh like nobody else ever could. When I was getting ready for service duty in the morning, I looked forward to seeing you. After service, I found myself smiling just thinking about the way you made me laugh so hard earlier in the day.

As we spent more time together, I learned more about you, and the more I learned, the more I liked you. You had such a genuinely sweet and kind heart, and I couldn't get enough of you. At the time, it was hard for me to admit that I was falling for you, and I denied it to my friends. But deep down, I knew I loved you.

My relationship with you was a breath of life. We spent real time together. And when I say real, you may be thinking, well, what kind of real is there? What I mean by real time is the kind of time where the point of being together was support, encouragement and fun. You showed me a playful kind of love. I'm grateful for that.

Each time I asked myself why I fell in love with you,
I would think about everything we talked about.
Your awesome wonderful stories about what you had done at school.
Things that hurt or scared you in the past.
And I would feel that feeling again.

How It Started

He was wearing a crisp blue, long-sleeved shirt tucked in jeans. He was not that tall. His hair was actually a bit annoying at first. There was no remarkable feature on his face. I have a thing for cute guys, but his face didn't get my attention. But overall, he looked handsome still.

Maybe it was the way he carried himself. Maybe it was sheer confidence. Plus, I like the guy who can easily pull together a presence that predominantly draws attention. Qualities like that are so rare nowadays. People tend to exert too much or too little effort to succeed with that. I think he just knew how to strike a balance between the two.

But, I did not fall in love with him the first time I saw him.

It's not every time I fall in love just by mere first, second or even third sight. Feelings work for me differently. I know it is typical, but I fell in love with the little things about him first before completely falling in love with him.

I fell in love with how he wittily told stories. I fell in love with how words cascaded out from his mouth whenever he shared stories he really loved with me or even with others. A lot of people love talking but only few do it the way he does.

I fell in love with how he rubbed his stomach. I just pictured it now and realized that I still find that gesture funny. When a guy touches his belly as though he is pregnant, it can be a sign of insecurity, but there's a good chance that it also means the guy is trying to get you to notice him. Farouq did that very well.

I fell in love with how he called my name. He called it with an accent. I fell in love with how he *differed* from me.

I fell in love with his presence. I fell in love with how he became a constant part of my life — as I woke up, as I got through the day, as I ended the night. I had no idea how to "unlove" his presence. I fell in love with the idea of him coming into my life and changing how my small world revolved.

He filled in the gaps, he rearranged things, he broke walls, and he taught me to break my own walls. I fell in love with him in so many little ways. And even though I can't write all of them here, I know that our love was not something that we stumbled into; it was an understanding we grew into.

Memorable Moments

It was Monday. Farouq and I were shopping for groceries at *SuperLife*. I looked like what I usually look like – beautiful. I was wearing a black fitted top on a pencil denim skirt with a pair of sandals. He was wearing a black shirt on a pair of denim trousers.

From the time we left the lounge together to the time we got to SuperLife, we had about five people tell us how good we looked together. We felt like a couple instantly.

Some people are basically honest. They will tell you the truth unless they have a reason to lie. When they say you look good together, they mean you are an attractive pair. In most cases, their assertions are based solely on appearance. It doesn't necessarily mean that you two would literally make a good couple — it's for you and the other person to decide whether or not you would make a good couple.

Farouq already decided.
He was silent.
I glanced at him.

He was looking at me then he turned away. With a smile planted on his face.

A smile of victory?

He grabbed my hand. He held me tightly for me to regain my balance.
It was the first time he held my hand.
I was falling in love. It hurt.

How It Ended

After NYSC, I saw our relationship in an entirely different light. I found myself having to try harder and harder to connect with Farouq, to be on the same wavelength. I started to become weary and cynical. I kept thinking that it was a phase, or a hiccup, or a post-graduation relationship rut.

Until one day, it hit me: It wasn't just a hiccup. We were different.

We had always *been* different. Our approach to God was different. Different faith. Different truth. Different directions.

Suddenly, I couldn't see us ever truly connecting in the real world. There was a distance between us, a chasm that was widening so rapidly that I was afraid I'd be swallowed up forever. I was exhausted from reaching over it.

I told him.
I told him the truth.

Then I saw his eyes filled with tears. I couldn't believe it. I had never seen him like that. He was the toughest man I had ever met. Now he was weak and falling apart before my very eyes, unable to find the right words to express how much he wanted me back.

It shook me to see him so soft. I hadn't expected it. He was never good at showing his feelings and he just took me by surprise.

I could barely hold it together for the rest of our conversation. Minutes after, I went straight home and I cried my heart out.

Lessons Learnt

I've discovered that ending a relationship is often like the movement of a cloud past the sun. Initially, it seems so cloudy, so dark, so hard to figure out why things aren't working anymore, and then the shift happens. The view becomes brighter; you get more clarity. You receive THE LIGHT.

I received the light. I saw things from a new perspective. I grew up. I grew up from being easily tossed about like waves and blown around by every wind.

As humans, our natural desires can easily lead us into a wrong and even dangerous position. Especially when we are young, it is easy to become so convinced that we have found the right one that our judgement becomes blurred if not blind.

The most important lesson, from a guy like Farouq is that you should not settle. Farouq was a fantastic guy, and any girl would be lucky (Oops! I don't like to use that word but it works better than blessed here) to have him. But staying with him was not God's will for me. I knew it.

Some relationships may not lead us away from a path of devotion to the Lord and obedience to His Word but they may not be God's perfect will for you. That something is good doesn't mean it is godly and that something is godly doesn't mean it is perfect.

When we settle, it's because we don't trust God enough. We don't trust that God is more romantic than we are; that God is the most passionate being there is (in fact, who sacrificed His only begotten son out of love for us), and who wants the absolute best for our lives. When we don't trust God, we commit the original sin of Adam and Eve all over again; we grasp the gift of knowledge rather than wait for God to give us the gift He's had for us all along.

I'm sure God watches us stumble through relationships, laughing and thinking, "Oh you of little faith. Why do you not trust me?"

PART THREE
The Real Deal
(As shared on amakamediadotcom)

People ask me why I talk so much about myself on the blog. And I tell them, "If I don't share my own story, no one else will".

2:59 PM · 04 Mar 18 · Twitter for Android

CHAPTER NINE

Dear Diary

"Heart Rays. . .giving out light."
- amakamedia.com

I have been compiling my thoughts, feelings, heartache, angst, memories, inspiration and joys with a passion and gusto all my life. It really wasn't a hard thing for me to do. Looking back, I realize that I have always been a maniac writer and I just know that NOW is the perfect time to tell my story —warts and all. I've always felt like I was *called* to write. To speak my truth. To lay it all out on the line. To be brave. To not hold back. To just do it.

As a blogger, I wrote about truth, my truth. I wrote with and in pain. And I wrote about pain itself. I wrote about grace and mercy. And hope. And darkness. And light.

In too many ways to count, blogging changed me and the way I LIVED life. Blogging taught me to be observant about the personal growth I was experiencing. It trained my mind to track the changes in my life and understand the lessons therein.

The more I blogged, the deeper the knowledge I had of myself. It's a beautiful thing.

Blogging served as a personal tool to keep records of my journey but somewhere along the line, it became less about me writing the story and more about the story changing me. Through blogging, I've learned to be more open and vulnerable, I've grown and healed through the experience of recycling my pain for something useful, and I've shifted my focus to others, enabling them to do the same.

I've been downright shocked by how God uses my mediocre story-telling skills for His glory. I've watched him take my stories and work in hearts and minds, and I couldn't be more grateful for the opportunities that blogging has given me to make His name great in my little corner of the internet, and even all over the world. I have selected a few of my blog posts for this section.

Dear Diary, I'm The Biggest Hypocrite Ever

That morning as I sat down and reflected on my struggles with sin, I wrote this:

I'm probably the biggest hypocrite who blogs. I act very religious and talk about loving God with all my heart, but I end up doing things that I'd be embarrassed to even admit.

I know I shouldn't do it, but I did.

I am now a mystery to myself. I don't even understand how I think. I am baffled by my own experience. I am driven by motives and urges I don't even understand, let alone control.

Why am I so apt to do the opposite of what I know I should do? Why am I so quick to lie? Why don't I love my neighbour right? Why am I so prone to wandering off the path the Lord has set before me?

I'm a Christian, and I'm a hypocrite.
I want to change.
I need a change.

God loves me, I know. But He hates what I am doing. And the reason He hates what I'm doing is because He knows just how much I am hurting myself by living this double life.

I want to stop hurting myself.
I want to stop.

Lord, help me . . .

Devil, Leave Me!

I couldn't think of one time when after I had prayed and fasted for days that the devil did not strike. And he seemed to know where exactly to hit me!

Maybe my love for God is not that deep. Why would a small thing like that just entangle me? Why did I fall so easily? Kai!

I would really like to ask the devil why he doesn't get bored or get tired of using the same modus operandi every time to trip people up. Ahan!

OK, maybe it doesn't do that to everybody. At least for me, he seems to have just ONE plan:

To distract me.

Each time I step out for God, he steps out big time for me. And he brings the distraction that causes the most damage.

Last month would have been the best month ever. I would have sung praises to God had I not been carried away by lustful thoughts and desires. That lust thing had me on. But it's all good. I am better for it now.

When the devil struck, I wish I could say I handled it righteously. I wish I could say I overcame the temptation. I wish I could say I never gave in to pleasing my flesh. But I can't lie.

I am not sure I want to lie because when you have decided to live out loud for God, you've gotta be REAL. Being a Christian requires you to live authentically. And I am being real here.

I failed.
I failed woefully.
It was all my fault. All mine.

I gave the ugly-looking, focus-stealing and life-wrecking big head a chance.

Just one chance, and he stole a lot from me.

You, devil, you!

Just thinking about it makes me really mad. This is me venting on my blog, and in doing this, I'm hoping that anyone reading this will not fall into the snare of the devil. The devil never gets tired. He will DO ANYTHING not to allow you to enjoy what God has given, is giving, and will give you.

Thank God for His grace that restores and His mercy that endures and His blood that cleanses.

See, that you passed with flying colours yesterday should not make you become too confident o. There are more tests, trials and temptations right in front of you. Especially if you are doing all you can to live for Christ. And most especially, if you have just scored a victory in any area of your life.

Devil, leave me!

Reading the title of this post actually cracks me up. Who am I trying to deceive? The devil can't leave me to shine. It's never going to happen. I'm a terror to him as long as I keep abiding in THE LIGHT and being THE LIGHT.

He will come again. Sure thing. But this time, I will NOT let down my guard in the mighty name of Jesus!

"Be alert. Be on your watch! Your enemy, the devil is going about like a roaring lion looking for someone to devour."

Sweetie, don't let the devil rub you off your blessings. Keep your eyes fixed on Jesus. Don't blink.

When I'm Weak, You Make Me Strong

Hot tears splashed down my cheeks as I had been listening to Bishop T. D Jakes' sermon on YouTube. I heard a word God used to answer a question in my heart. At that moment, God's intentions leaped off the screen and started a revolution in me.
I wept and wept.

I never would have guessed how highly God thinks of me. I never would understand how invaluable I am to His kingdom. I felt a strange combination of exhilaration and anxiety about what it would mean to be called a strong woman.

This truth caused me hours and hours of tears. This truth tore me apart inside, ripping at the falsehood I had worn and adorned, shredding my self-made safety nets, and leaving me very broken and helpless.

I gasped for breath as I come face to face with what's real.

What is real is that I need Him.

Without Jesus, I will face the wrath of a Just God who cannot tolerate sin.

I needed help desperately.

And there is a God who says that in Him I can be strong.

Without Jesus, I am nothing. Nothing at all.

And without this great struggle that leaves me gasping for breath, I would have completely missed Him. Instead, I would have clung to the image I had created and never been forced to look at Him as He truly is.

I serve a God who is greater than my struggles,
but I would not have known this if I had not stumbled through them.

I serve a God who brings victory to the darkest of defeats,
but I would not have known this if I didn't crawl through darkness.

I serve a God who miraculously breathes new life into the ugly and broken, but I
would not have known this if I never looked honestly at my own
weaknesses.

And most of all, I serve a God who *"investigates my life, finds out everything
about me; cross-examines me and tests me, to get a clear picture of what I'm about.
. . then guide me on the road to eternal life."* (Psalm 139:23-24, MSG)

And I am very, very thankful.

I am thankful because there is a much deeper truth about this experience.

Dear Diary, I'm in The Middle of a War

Every day I'm in a battle.

The prize? My attention. My time. My priorities. And most valuable of all,
my heart.

My enemy is cunning and crafty with many tried and true weapons at his
disposal. His favourites — schedules, conflict, busyness, social media,
men. Each of these he knows very well and plans skillfully.

He also knows he doesn't need to attack me with all of them at once. If he
could use just one to successfully invade and conquer the territory of my
heart, his mission will be accomplished. My heart, distracted.

Someone whose heart is torn into two doesn't know what to believe or
how to act. A distracted person will never be a light-bearer for Christ
because a distracted person is not a powerful person. That's not the person
I want to be.

I will fight to protect the fire. I will fight to stay in the light. I will fight to
live out the truth. I will fight for my peace and wholeness. I will fight!

It would have been a hopeless, helplessly lost battle, if not for one thing:

God has invested so much in me. I am armed too.

My weapons? The Word of God, the angelic armies of the Most High, and a mighty weapon that is as unlikely as it is deadly - time spent sitting quietly at my Lover's feet. It is this defense that gives me the armor I need to fight the enemy (For I do not wrestle against flesh and blood). This is why, before he can unleash his attack, I would have run to my Creator with these words on my lips:

"Lord, give me a heart burning only for You."
Only for You.

It's not an easy thing to be.

I've discovered that one effective way of protecting the territory of my heart is: STAYING IN THE SECRET PLACE. When I take the time to clear my mind of all distractions and fix my eyes solely on Christ, I find that He gives me a greater joy and peace than anything else ever can.

It's not been easy, really. There were days I felt too tired to read my Bible; times when I thought skipping my personal prayer time and jumping right into my day would be more productive. There were moments when I struggled to be still before my Heart Keeper. But I've learned that whenever I feel this way, I'm in the middle of a battle.

When I don't give in to the devil and instead press more into God, that's when He profoundly speaks to my heart and gives me a fresh measure of peace, passion, and power.

Is it hard to just sit in God's presence when all the things (sewing, blogging, chatting, etc) I have to do are calling me? Yes. But it's totally, absolutely and wonderfully worth it.

P.S I'll be away for a few more days. My heart cries for more. I don't want to be distracted.

I challenge you today to stop and simply delight in the presence of God. Quieten the noise, and let His peace wash over you. Strip yourself of every weight, and let him breathe into you.

Stay inspired.

My Break-Free from an Unequally Yoked Relationship

Right at the beginning, I knew the relationship was headed for destruction.

I never wanted to get into that relationship and so wanted to get out of it the moment I got into it. However, I let my emotions lead me and ultimately control me! It was the deadliest place I've ever been in my life!!! I not only lost myself, but I also got chained up. In a cage.

I was not his girlfriend and he was not going to marry me but we had a *connection*. Connection, was the preferred word for our relationship.

We served on the same team. Our first one-on-one communication was when he reached out to me on the phone; he asked me a work-related question. And that one phone call led to other phone calls. I was totally not interested in him because he wasn't anywhere close to getting married. At least, he was open about that one. Besides, he didn't have ANY of the core qualities I wanted in a husband, but I did find him attractive *sha*.

Prior to him coming into my life, I was single and really didn't have any friend (so it seemed in my mind because the devil threw a lie at me and I bought it). So, I was lonely and needed someone to call mine.

I pretty much gave up hope that God would bless me with the one He had for me. *Smh*. Since this guy was available at the time, I settled and agreed to be his girlfriend. It was the biggest mistake I ever made.

I was his girlfriend and not his girlfriend. Confused? Me too. I was his girlfriend because we talked, hung out and did stuff but I wasn't his girlfriend because no one knew about our relationship. We could not even introduce each other as friends and he never wanted us to be seen together by family and friends. At a point, it was as if he was ashamed of me and tried to keep me in hiding.

He was my secret sin.

Each time I got out of the relationship, he ran after me pleading to get back my attention. Yet, he would never love me right when I went back. Since he didn't know what love was, he didn't know how to properly love me. He gave more attention to his work (as he always claimed to be busy), and other things that I had to practically fight to get his attention.

I realized I was in a hot mess when I still stayed even after I found out he had been speaking/spending time with another girl (now I'm even thinking he had many girlfriends). If I confronted him with evidence, he would just flat out lie to my face with no remorse. This, of course, made me feel devastated as if I experienced a death.

The relationship had me living in a circle (or is it cycle?). Running out and going back in, running out and going back in.

And I wanted to TOTALLY break free because I felt stuck in that relationship for quite some time.

I fasted. I prayed. Ah.

I just couldn't explain nor understand how and why I crawled back into the relationship every single time.

Since I was being pushed farther away from my personal relationship with God, my world became revolved around him. Over time, I realize I didn't actually love him but I loved the things we did together. I was addicted to being around him every week.

I was willing to sacrifice my calling to be with him. It was that bad.

When he ignored me, I felt unworthy. I felt useless without him. He knew he was driving me crazy and seemed to be enjoying it. I couldn't share my frustration with anyone because nobody knew about us.

I forgot my identity. My worth. I almost lost me.

I wasted so much energy trying to have him around me all the time, trying to win his love and attention. I was unhappy and drowning in my own misery. Ah, I wasted so much valuable time mehn!

Throughout our relationship, he would seek to receive more than give. The more I would give, the more empty I was left.

My freedom started when God showed me the truth and filled my void. He showed me that true love cannot be earned, it is freely given. It's not based on the things I do or who accepts me, but on who I am.

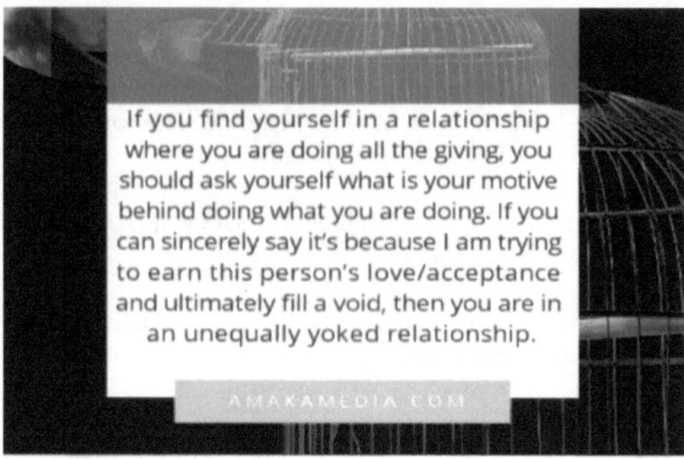

The relationship was torture. Dysfunction. Narcissism.

We hardly agreed on anything! It was a constant battle of the wills. To please God or not to please God.

After all, it is the Spirit of God that unites two people. Anything contrary to the Spirit of God will bring about division. We were headed in two different directions and were never going to meet because we did not share the same beliefs, goals, passions, vision, principles, convictions, etc. Most importantly, our relationship lacked PURPOSE. Therefore, even though we were together, we did not walk together towards the same purpose - Christ.

True love is shown through ACTIONS. A godly man will commit himself to the lady he loves and be committed to showing his love to her. There will be no doubt, confusion, or questioning of his love for her. She will know that she is loved and accepted because of WHO SHE IS, not what she does. Nothing will cause their love towards you to lessen because it will be pure and true.

I am SO glad that God renewed my hope in Him, gave me the strength and courage to cut that relationship off, and showed me that TRUE LOVE is only found in HIM. Only HE can fill our voids. I am SO thankful that I made the decision to LET GO and have received the power to LOVE and OBEY GOD.

I am free indeed!

Thank God I Am Not Married Yet

Lord, I am sincerely grateful that I have not walked down the aisle yet. I would have married prematurely . . .

Lord, thank You for saving me from the path of destruction. I almost gave in due to pressure.

Lord, my perceptions have changed through this time. My confidence has grown tremendously. I am a better woman because of You.

Lord, I am grateful for the lessons You are teaching me in this period of waiting. There is no better time to learn about them than now.

Lord, I know You are not only working in me, but also working in my future hubby right at this minute. And I believe You will make us meet when we're fully ready.

Lord, I am really happy about the wisdom I have found in Your word as regards to marriage so far. I never would have forgiven myself if I was married before now. Thank You so so much!

Lord, I'm grateful for this season. I am enjoying how You are opening my eyes to clearly see the paths of your purpose for my marriage, my ministry and my life in general.

Lord, thank You for the grace bestowed upon me. Help me to utilize the gift and blessing of singlehood. Help me to forget the past and look forward to what lies ahead.

I choose to trust Your plans for my marital destiny. And so I lay down every weight of depression, loneliness, frustration, and discontentment from my heart in the name of Jesus.

Heavenly Father, today I sincerely thank You that I am not yet married!

I know my days of being single are numbered. However, at the moment, I'm having the best time of my life!

This Is The Woman I See

I am so excited about the woman I am growing into. I love her crazily. I admire her values, goals, priorities and every single thing that makes her an exceptional person.

The woman I see is a sweetheart to many and God. She is one of God's favourites. She is a strategic instrument in His hands.

The woman I see is a threat to the kingdom of darkness. It can't stand the glory she carries. It can't comprehend the intensity of light in her. She is powerful!

I see me, a woman who is taking over territories and leading nations.

I see me, a woman who speaks so that many may be blessed and delivered from the bondage of sin, failures and poverty.

Ah, the woman I see is rich.

She feeds thousands.

She lends to nations.

The woman I see is actually not perfect. She has her flaws. Her looks might not stop you dead in your tracks but her confidence and personality will, her cooking might not send you places you've never been - neither will her voice nor her writing - but this woman I am becoming, she is one heck of a phenomenal woman!

I see me, an African woman. A strong woman. A woman who is growing strong with each disappointment, each challenge, each heartbreak, and each victory.

I see me, a woman who is more authentic, more satisfied, and more committed to being who God wants her to be.

I see me, a woman who stands out from the crowd. She is not standing out based on what she wears but who and whose she is.

I see me, a woman sitting with kings and presidents. She is among those whose names constantly make the headlines.

Ah, the woman I see is a celebrity.

The woman I see is not ordinary. She is not sitting and folding her hands. She is creating businesses for other businesses. She is making things happen. She is just too much!

The Woman I See

I see me, the woman who lives for God, who carries a grace that only a relationship with Him brings and a light that only shines out of an intimate relationship with God.
I see me, a woman who others want to be associated with, not because of what she has, but because she exudes God from her very breath.
I see me; the lioness who isn't scared to believe every of God's word spoken to her • • •

The woman I see carries a grace that only shines out of an intimate relationship with God. The woman I see is passionate about God. She loves God. She breathes God.

I see me, a woman whose husband looks at every morning and praises God. She is a "good thing" to her husband.

I see me, a woman whose husband adores, loves and respects. She loves and supports her husband. She is a fantastic helpmeet.

speaks in tongues

I see . . .
I see . . .
I see . . .

The woman I see is far greater, stronger and wiser than the woman I am now. I am learning and growing to become the woman I see . . .

CHAPTER TEN

Dealing with Heartbreak

"Only when the vase is cracked, can light get out."
- John Green

Currently experiencing a heartbreak?

My advice to you is to truly be kind to yourself in this very painful state. Please be compassionate with yourself. You are perfect in every way you are and I know it is very dark and challenging right now, but you can get through this. You will get through this. I fully understand those words are not what you want to read, but you are not alone.

Whatever the current situation is you are experiencing right now, know that everything indeed does happen for a reason, whether you choose to believe it or not, and there is a lesson behind it you will see in retrospect. Be patient with yourself and learn more about you. Time doesn't heal; it is wisdom that does. Discover the greatest lesson in the shortest time possible.

My biggest advice to you from my heart is to trust that everything is going to be okay. Be resilient. Feel your feelings, but do not allow them to suffocate you.

You are in control here, sweetheart. *Trust yourself. Trust God.*

If I never would have believed in the internal strength I had, I never would have gotten through the past relationships. I never realized how good life could be until I stopped letting myself hold me back. The most important thing you can do is believe in yourself and believe in your strength. Sometimes, when you're willing to accept your strength, it allows you to appreciate your past.

Ten Things I'd Say to Someone Going Through a Heartbreak

1. Do not regret the experience. Look deeply to find the beauty and the lesson from the pain.

2. Be careful who you share your painful story with. Put your dignity and integrity in check.

3. Take things one day at a time. Try not to look too far into the future. Slowly, steadily work through each day.

4. Manage your money. Don't go on a shopping spree to get over the ache. It will do you no good. Save for rainy days.

5. Take care of yourself. Eat healthy food. Don't forget to smile. It looks like the world has ended, but each day is still a gift.

6. Create your own world. Make it a happy one. Take charge of your emotions.

7. Appreciate the people who love, support, and help you. They are trying the best they can to share in your pain.

8. Leave your ex in the past. A part of you would love to check his/her photos on social media, but move on. Stop double-clicking on your past. Again, move on!

9. Bless someone. The best time to be a blessing is when you are heartbroken. Our burdens feel lighter when we help another.

10. Forgive the one who hurt you. Forgiveness brings you the healing you need. It unlocks you from the prison of your past and sets you free.

What to Do When He Ignores You

The first thing you need to know is never to degrade yourself or lose your respect. Whether you are being given all the attention in the world or being ignored does not in any way change who you are.

Firstly, let me tell you why he might ignore you, or I should say why I was ignored. These are a few possible reasons:

- It was a casual friendship. And suddenly, you are becoming way too serious about it.
- He has started to grow feelings for you. He is scared you might not like him the same way.

- It might be his general behaviour. When he notices you are getting too close to him, it freaks him out and pushes him away.
- He has noticed some negative traits or red flags about you.
- He probably told you about it, but you have refused to improve on yourself.
- He might not be aware he is ignoring you or that you are worried he is not talking to you.
- He probably has other things to focus on and has gotten his mind too occupied (I have done that many times).
- He is probably seeing someone.

Don't go assuming you know why they are ignoring you though. Ask questions. Talk to them about it. Let out how you feel.

Whatever their reasons, always remember that:

The Reason Won't Change Your Life.

I said it before. I am saying it again. Whether people like you or not does not affect who you are.

Whatever reason he gives, don't push it. The harder you try to hold his closer, the further they're going to push you away.

Once you've asked him, don't ask again. The more you ask why he's ignoring you, the more lighthearted or hurtful comments you might get.

Worse, he may even laugh and lie to your face! *"What?! No, I'm not ignoring you! I've just been erm . . . busy . . . you know . . . ?!"*

Can you ever feel more foolish?
Move on.

Easier said than done, right?
I know you'd say that!
Let me give you a little background of my story:

I was not very popular in school, I was shy and timid. I was ignored a lot as a child. I struggled with an inferiority complex and low self-esteem. I grew up fighting back to get attention. I craved for attention. I wanted a lot of it! When people ignored me, I felt miserable. . . sad. I hated it.

I know that sometimes people can't always get back to you right away. I understand and I'm cool with that. And it's not like I want them to reply my every post or message or anything like that. It's not that I want attention all the time. If someone (for example) doesn't want to talk, it's fine to say, "I can't talk right now!"

But when someone I know well is obviously deliberately ignoring me, I get anxiety attacks. I can't stand it, especially if I don't know what I did or said to upset the person. And it makes me really angry.

Because I didn't want to be miserable every time, I needed to find a way around it. So I did.

Now I can tell you this is what you should do:

1. Accept the fact: Whatever might be the reason, don't be miserable about it. Do not be all clingy. Accept the fact with dignity and with as much grace as you can. Blow their minds with the grace actually. Leave them alone and stay on your own lane. Smile at them if you happen to have an eye contact with them, but keep walking ahead. (if you are a lady, do the catwalk. Lol). Don't try talking to them whenever you get a chance. Make them believe that you are happy in your own world, without them.

2. Love yourself: I have tried and tested it. You must love yourself if you want people to love you. See how wonderful and graceful you are. Not everybody is able to handle situations so nicely as you do. You are awesome. Be proud and know you are lovable. Don't let anybody make you feel miserable. If not for anything else, for the fact that God *killed* his only son just for you! Such love.

3. Be mind-blowing: Heart breaks are the most effective triggers to make people do great things. Do something special not to attract them but in general. Something to showcase your great, strong, wonderful self to the world. You have a lot of potential . . . use it . . . do something wonderful with it. Go about your business.

4. Look good every single time: Looking your best as much as you can will have an impact on more things you can imagine. The way you look is the reflection of your whole personality. There is no way you will not be noticed when you look good. Even if you are feeling like just there . . . always . . . always make a pretty picture. Don't wear the stress on your face. Smile, laugh and look awesome!

Yes, smile often. It doesn't matter if the smile is fake. Just don't frown. :)

5. Encourage someone: I reserved the best for the last. Find somebody going through depression or loneliness and speak words of encouragement to that person. The Bible says in 1 Thessalonians 5:14 (CEV); "Encourage anyone who feels left out, help all who are weak, and be patient with everyone." Instead of looking inward and allowing neglect to eat away at you, turn outward and use God's grace in your life to serve others; it's ministry, it's powerful, and it makes a difference. Doing this will not only change their lives, but yours as well.

So sweetie, stop being worried that you are being ignored. Shift your focus from those ignoring you and focus on GOD, YOU and YOUR PURPOSE (the dream). Let it also be a good opportunity for you to rediscover yourself.

When He Chooses the Other Girl Over You

I am not psychic and cannot look into your individual situation. But what I
can do is try to shed some light for you so that you can understand.

It won't be too long before it dawns on you that some guys don't know
what they want or need. And you can't know what a man needs or wants
when he has you, yet chooses someone else over you.

Instead of worrying yourself and driving yourself crazy about the
awkward situation, the best thing for you to do would be to MOVE ON.

That's the hard part - moving on.
I'm starting to dislike that phrase.

I didn't know how hard it is to move on until my *friend* got a girlfriend
without letting me know. I saw the signs but I kept on asking questions
and giving him many chances to tell the truth. He never did.

They say the truth hurts. But, something hurts more - a lie thrown at your
face.

You feel foolish.
You feel unworthy.
You feel rejected.
You want to fight back.

"Why did he choose her over me?" you ask yourself many times over.

Then you start thinking about proving to him why he should have chosen you instead. Forget it. It's not worth it.

Wait a minute, what were you even going to do? I know right.

You go on social media and stalk her. You want to know about her, what she looks like. You want to try to understand what makes a man choose one woman over another. When you see her, you realize you are smarter than her, look better than her, and you feel you are obviously the best choice.

Then you start to ask more questions:

What does he see in her?
Why did he choose her?
What does she have that I don't have?
Is something wrong with me?

See, the mere fact that he considered another person over you is enough to pick yourself up, adjust what's necessary and move on.

The first thing you must do is to understand the relationship mannerism of the man. For example, if the guy is only dating you and not looking to be serious, then he is always going to hop around from woman to woman and there is no reason trying to wreck your heart to figure out why he is choosing another woman over you. That's obviously his pattern. There is always going to be another woman for him to choose because that is how he is. The issue is him and NOT YOU.

The second thing you must do is to RUN back to God. See things through God's eyes. What if He was trying to save your life from a wreck? What if God had seen the end from the beginning (as He always does). A man's rejection could be God's promotion. Trust that.

It really doesn't matter why he chose her. All that matters is that he is no longer your problem.

Don't waste valuable time trying to figure it out. It will just make you jealous and sad. You might end up doing stupid things (that you would regret later)

Here's what I did: I copied the other girl's number from his phone and saved it for an "in case something goes wrong" situation. When something eventually went wrong and our friendship went sour, I checked out her photos and called her to confirm my suspicions. *Stupid*! The issue escalated and I hadn't felt stupid-er after that.

Sweetie, if he chooses you over some girl, I am writing to you. It's just sad that I had to go through certain things before I understood them or even thought of sharing on the blog.

Here are a few suggestions:

- He is not thinking about you. Don't fool yourself and waste your time thinking that he is.
- Don't diminish yourself by playing second to a man that did not choose you as his number one. Thank God and consider it a blessing. When He moves something out of your way; it's usually to make way for something better!
- Don't trick yourself into thinking that you can change his mind. He has made his choice, allow him to stick with his decision. Begging and pleading for explanations just makes you look desperate. *And desperation looks ugly.*
- Know your worth! You are valuable, just because someone else does not appreciate that does not change that.
- You will never be able to move forward with your life if you continue to live in the past. Rehashing and reviewing this situation over and over again is just a waste of time.
- Dry your tears and move forward. You never know what is waiting for you around the corner.

Go outside. Do some of your favourite activities that you've been neglecting lately, or didn't get a chance to do in the relationship. Start going out to see your friends again out in public at the park, or the mall, or the church.

This is only a page in your book, it is not the end. Release. Heal. Start to plan for the next chapter.

CHAPTER ELEVEN
The Healing Process

"However deep the pit, God's love is deeper still."
- Corrie Ten Boom

As I reflect on my life, the way I loved and was loved before I started on my journey to wholeness, I'm amazed I got to this point in one piece (or, should I say peace?). The person I used to be seems like a very bad dream. God intervened many times to keep me from self-destruction, I'm convinced.

There is no point sugarcoating it. The healing process can be messy and painful, but oh, it is so worth it.

Anyone who gets on the other side of the healing path will feel the same way. The world just feels different. You see things differently. And you understand people differently too.

An author once described the examination and cutting out process as "walking through cleansing fire." I guess it is an accurate description of recovery and healing. When the journey starts, it can feel a lot like tearing the mask off our faces and tearing our hearts open — once it's started, there is no turning back.

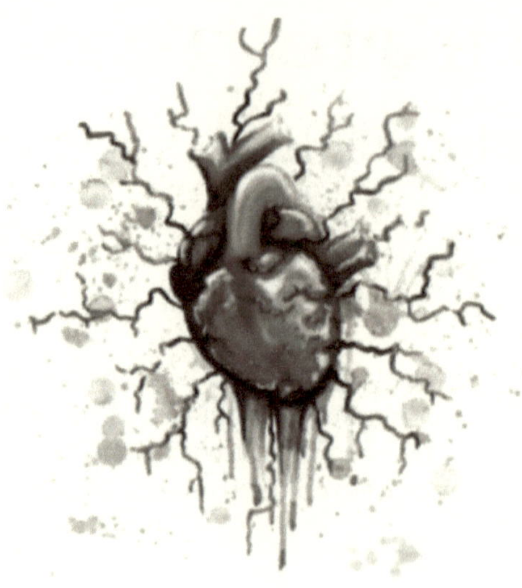

Betrayal, rejection, sin, had cut me to my core. And the wounds were still open. My heart was bleeding with pain.

The story about the woman with the issue of blood recorded in the Bible became truth for me. Her story pierced my heart in the way that it brought me to tears . . . to Jesus.

She had been bleeding for 12 long years!

"If I can just touch the hem of his garment, I will be healed". That's what she told herself. Such a daring adventure.

Like her, I needed healing too.
"He can heal me too!!!" she declared.
She was desperate.
She must get to Jesus.

And in a moment of inspiration, it occurred to her, "This man, this Jesus, is a great healer".

"Maybe if I could just TOUCH HIM."

Maybe if she could quietly make her way through the crowd and touch the hem of his garment, then she might be healed.

After everything she had been through—twelve long years of lonely, painful suffering—she held on tightly to the faith that this man named Jesus could make her whole.

I could relate with this woman for a minute. Just a minute. You can imagine having that issue of blood every day of your life for 12 years.

That's 4,383 days.
144 months.
624 weeks.
105,192 hours.

For 12 years, the woman bore the emotional and psychological baggage of being unclean and untouchable.

- No cuddling
- No true relationship
- No sex (if she was married)
- She could not prepare food for her family (if she even had one)
- She could not do house chores
- She couldn't be a wife
- She couldn't be a mother
- She had lived in an isolated house for 12 long years staring at the walls

For all intents and purposes, she was as good as dead

And with a single word from Jesus, 12 long years of pain were swept away:

"Daughter . . . your faith has made you whole."
Just like that!
Just like that?! Not really. It was a process.

She made the effort. She went past the piercing eyes and whispering lips. She ignored the stares and the what-ifs. She reached out.

I reached out to Jesus.
He took me on a journey.

The journey was a long stretch. I got on the other side, but it was three steps forward and two steps back most of the time. Yet every step of the way gleaned new understanding and developed new insight for immediate use. There came the realization that every stumble and setback was worth it, because this path led directly to God.

The walk became less of the world and less of me, but more with God. Surrendering to His wisdom and control made it easier, quicker. The path became more about taking charge of choices.

I might have never gotten to the perfect destination. My challenges and issues might not have ended. What changed was my perception of things that happen, my ability to process them, and my expression throughout. The things that would make me feel broken and ashamed no longer had the same effect.

Healing is painful. Growth is painful. Change is painful. But nothing is as painful as staying stuck somewhere you don't belong.

It can be lonely but it's not a ride I take alone, because God is with me through all the peaks and valleys. He wants me to find my life, my movement, and my being in Him.

This beautiful and famous recovery prayer by Reinhold Niebur captures everything about this journey to wholeness:

"God, grant us the serenity to accept the things we cannot change, the courage to change the things we can and the wisdom to know the difference."

I'd like to paraphrase it this way:

Dear Holy Spirit, I cannot live for even a day without You. Help me. Teach me. I surrender my life and my weaknesses to You . . .

Grant me the serenity to accept the things I have no control over — other people, their thoughts, feelings, and actions.

Grant me the courage to change only the things I can change — my perception, my character, my heart.

Grant me the wisdom every day to know the difference between the truth and the pull of the flesh. I ask in the name of Jesus. Amen.

CHAPTER TWELVE

Taking The 30-Day Man Fast

"Life stings but stings don't last forever. His love does."
- Bola 'Salt' Essien-Nelson

Are you sick and tired of failing in your relationships? Are you always relationship hopping and constantly trying to fill voids?

Do you spend your nights on meaningless and purposeless dates with boys who bore you or have nothing to offer? Are you sick of having guys take up so much of your mental space and time? Take a fast.

God says: Take a break from men to solely focus on me for 30 days and see what I will do (Your fast might be longer or shorter).

Sometimes it's hard to discover your true purpose and identity when you are always attached or involved with someone else. Can you take a break?

This is not saying men are evil or distractions. This is also not a "Girl, you don't need a man, be an independent woman" type of blog post. I am not telling you to leave the man in your life if you are in a God-ordained, loving relationship.

However, this is a very personal one for me. Most of my posts are generally *personal* anyway, because I am either writing out of experience, through a biblical discovery or from deep thoughts in my heart.

This was laid in my heart a couple of months ago. But I have not FULLY obeyed. Something tells me I don't feel accountable because I have not shared it with you yet. So this is me telling you what I would be doing for a month (which might extend to the end of the year as the Spirit leads):

I AM TAKING A MAN FAST

Men are my weakness. They are my biggest distraction. I tend to be an emotional wreck over *any type* of relationship that never works, which in turn leaves me questioning whether I have a problem. I go from being confident and focused to feeling depressed, lonely and unloved. I was at the beginning of a new relationship when I realized I had hit a low point already. I unknowingly desperately needed something different than what I had experienced, and I knew only God could fix me.

At a point, I was dealing with rejection issues, because it seemed like somehow in all my relationships I was either rejected or taken for granted at the end of the day. This is probably not completely accurate, but that's how I felt when things didn't work out. I'm like: *"God why is Your presence not helping me through this. Why do I keep going around this redundant mountain of dysfunctional relationships?"*

I spent time talking to God about "my unfortunate relationships", expressly pouring my heart content to Him. I was honest and totally desperate for Him to make me whole.

God is so loving, I tell you. He heard me and told me things I never knew about myself and my journey. Among all the things He whispered, He asked that I go off the relationship radar for a month.

"A month. Sure!"

It sounded so easy but every time I tried to do this fast, it ended up after two weeks.

Within two weeks of no man - just God and I - I'd feel so high-spirited and whole, because God would show me just how complete His love is, and all I needed to do was trust in His love. He would tell me how beautiful He has made me and how gifted I am. That's when I boldly declare *"I'm Single And Free!"*, *"I'm Complete In Christ!"* etc.

Then, while basking in the half-baked euphoria of my new sense of identity, purpose and freedom, I would go back again or meet someone new. There was always a Jerry, a Mr. Man or a boy coming around. This went on and on and on.

"Oh no. Why can't I stay without talking to a man for just a month? Just a month!"

I have become too tired of my weakness and can no longer continue this way.

This fast is to learn how to place God above everything else . . . man, especially.

So by writing to myself, I hope it speaks to you too.

Why You Should Take the Fast

You already have an idea about why I need this fast. How about you?

What if this fast is the only way to draw closer to God, and to hear more clearly from Him. Would you not do it?

What if this fast is to teach you how to totally surrender yourself to God and allow him to heal the parts of your life that are wounded. Would you not do it?

What if this fast is the way to GROW into maturity in your relationship with God. Would you not do it?

What if this fast is the only thing you have to do to make all your dreams come true. Would you not do it?

I definitely would!

How to Take The Fast

After doing it my own way and failing over and over, with God's help I came up with these guidelines:

<u>Guideline 1</u>
STOP all communication with any man who you presume to be a love interest or who has the characteristics you desire. Stay clear of any man you're dating/talking to that's leading nowhere, especially if you know God has given you signs that this person is not for you and you have no peace about the relationship.

<u>Guideline 2</u>
DO NOT engage or entertain any man who is trying to be friends with you, flirt with you, or take you out on a date. Even if a friend tries to match you up with a guy, stay away.

If you are a beautiful woman (which I know you are), men will always come. You must stay aware!

This is the weakest area for me because they always come. Remember when I cried out *"Devil, leave me alone!"* the other day? Yeah. That was exactly what happened!

It is not something to brag about but God is my witness, EVERY TIME I decide to take on a man fast, a guy would just show face. At first I thought it was cute, but then it dawned on me that it was no coincidence, that even the devil knows about the season I'm totally dedicated to God. I have come to understand that this fast is indeed something VERY crucial for me to do in order to fulfil my God-given dreams and purpose. The energy and time I'm consistently squandering away in the pursuit of love and attention are distracting me too much from what God plans to do in my life this season. I really need this break, to break away from the pattern . . . to sustain focus.

I need it!

Guideline 3

DO NOT give in into the temptation to take another cute guy's phone number or give out yours with the thought that you will start talking with them after the fast. Don't, even if he says it's strictly business.

This is important because every time you choose to reject advances from men, you are obeying God. Each rejection is an act of faith. And you know that faith without good works is dead. Right?

If you want to be polite, tell them that you are not into dating for now. *Take this fast seriously. It's a delicate season.*

So I beg you, if you are going to do this, stay committed.

Wait, Are You Saying I Should Not Talk To Any Man?

No. That's not what I mean. Of course, we can't live without talking to men. However, be VERY aware of the men you talk to during this period. Stick to:

1. **Friends**: Men who are already platonic friends. No new friends.

2. **Colleagues**: If it is essential for your job, of course. BUT avoid contact with male co-workers who try to make advances at you, or colleagues you feel some sort of likeness for.

3. **Relatives**: Sure, you can talk to your father, brother, uncle, cousins. BLOOD-RELATED guys.

4. **Church Members**: Let every discussion be about God, church activities/meetings and nothing more!

5. **No crush**: I say again, no crush. The devil is so tricky *ehn*. This is when that bros you have been crushing on will now come and say "Hello beautiful". Run!

<u>**Guideline 4**</u>

Keep a record of every feeling, thought, and revelation you get in each day of this fast. You may write, take photos or even record videos to document your experience. Just pour out freely. This will help you SEE how much you have grown and been changed.

Sweetie, I want to encourage you to take on a man fast too. This fast is important, because you are showing God that you are willing to sacrifice your desires for His purpose in your life.

The man that's for you will always be yours. Why not obey God first?

Some Diary Entries During My Fast

A number of my blog readers requested that I keep them updated on my 30-Day Man Fast. I shrugged at it because I considered it to be a personal journey between God and I. Then again, I thought to share moments that weren't creepily sacred.

Day 1: Does This Make Any Sense?

I grabbed my diary, Bible and a pen as if I was expecting God to suddenly start dictating for me to write.

I didn't even know what I was supposed to do.

I started to cry.

I shed tears for about 15 minutes.

After a while, I decided that since it was the first day of the fast, I should write what I intend to achieve at the end.

I wrote out five objectives:
- To learn how to be independent in body, soul and spirit as a single woman by totally depending on God (Wholeness).
- To learn how to put God above everything else . . . and everyone else (Focus).
- To be satisfied with Jesus only (Contentment).
- To be fixed - that my broken past and experience shall be unto God's glory (Recovery).
- To know and understand God's purpose for my life in this season (Clarity).

Thereafter, a song popped up in my mind. I hummed it, then sang it softly a few times. And sang it even more passionately.

It was Mary Mary's I try. The lyrics came alive in my spirit:

I should know by now there's no way no
How I could live my life without you
Still I get caught up in myself
And talk to you less and less
And every time that I do
I come right back to you
Cause after all my mistakes
I know that I have to change
So I put my life in your hands

I wish I could undo some things that
I have done in my past
But I can't erase what's already taken place
So from now on I'll try to do my best
Cause after all my mistakes
I know that I have to change
So I put my life in your hands
I try but sometimes I fail
Now I realize that I need your help
Cause I can't make it all by myself
I need you

It was a perfect description of my Heart Rays at the time. I had realized I couldn't go any further without God. I needed to surrender it all.

I also sang Don Moen's River of Love over and over again:
Thirsty for more you
More of your Spirit and truth
Wash me from all my sin
Fill me with your Spirit again

You're the river of love
Flowing with the grace and mercy
Flooding my soul
Filling my heart with peace
O river of love
Like streams in the desert
Giver of life
Giving your life and love

To set me free

Thereafter, it felt like God was responding to my heart:

"I love you, Amaka. My love for you runs deep like a river. I come to give you life, love and light."

I felt good. Really good.

Then I listened to Joseph Prince on YouTube. I can't remember the title of the message but it blessed me. He talked about how we can lean on God's love and not worry about anything. He said something that has stuck with me:

"It is better to boast on God's love for you than boast on your love for Him. Because while your love can grow cold, God's love is constant."

I felt better. Refreshed. Loved.

I have been trying too hard to earn God's love because I had forgotten that nothing I do can reduce or increase the magnitude of love He already has for me.

I breathed out anxiety from my heart and breathed in the love of God. Then I prayed for grace to always bask in His Love.

God loves me. That's all that matters to me right now.

***

That was Day 1.

This fast has been a life-altering journey. It seems like God is opening my heart and making me take a look inside. I am amazed at myself.

You might think it's crazy I am taking this fast and choosing not to talk to men for 30 days but God has really been showing me some powerful things about myself. I'd recommend it for every single woman to do it at least once in her life.

Personally, this fast is mainly about staying away from distractions (men) and getting back to the heart of God and my purpose. I also don't want to start a new relationship without first dealing with my inner man.

I still have some days to go. Slowly, but surely I will get there.

Day 9: I Am Hungry for Love

I had a great encounter with God through His word. It was like when Jesus sat down with the Samaritan woman by the well.

He addressed my deepest need by initiating a conversation, "Would you give me a drink?"

Lovingly, He steered the conversation through a territory that explored the many ways I had tried to satisfy my own emptiness, including failed relationships, illicit pleasures, and empty religiosity.

"You don't miss Him. You only miss the idea of having someone in your life."

At about 6PM, I had a strong desire to pick up my phone and call someone. I wanted to hear something like "I miss you".

It's been days without talking to me, is he not missing me? Why hasn't he tried to call? I fought the feeling with raging thoughts. I actually told him bluntly that I needed to stay away from him. I was wondering where this feeling of wanting him to call came from. *Let's blame the devil.*

I started to think of a good reason to call him. Maybe asking him to help me out with a project would work. I picked up my phone but . . . I couldn't dial.

I fought the feeling. Oh I fought!

Calling him would be an act of disobedience as the fast demands that I do not call, text or care about any man for 30 days.

I started to cry. My soul cried out to God.

Fix me, Lord . . .
Fill me, Lord . . .
Fill me, Lord . . .
Let Your love fill this void in my heart.
Satisfy me, Jesus.

In moments like these, I sing out a song or listen to one that speaks to my spirit. This time, it was Alvin Slaughter's Who Can Satisfy My Soul.

Who can satisfy my soul, like You
Who on earth can comfort me and love me like You do
Who could ever be more faithful and true
I will trust in You, I will trust in You, my God

As I sang, He made a staggering offer:

"If you look to Me for satisfaction, you will find your deepest needs and longings met. Will you?"

I am now looking unto Jesus. Only He can satisfy my deep hunger for love and attention. It's only Him.

Instead of seeking your satisfaction in stuff, in men and other ephemerals, will you turn your heart to Jesus and receive His eternally thirst-quenching, soul-satisfying gift of living water?

Join me to experience the deep, genuine love and joy that has captured my heart like the woman at the well.

Day 30: I Choose Jesus

My prayer during this fast has been for God to fix me, fill me, change me so I don't make the same mistakes I've made in my past relationships.

I was sowing time and energy into relationships that just weren't working. I had become so frustrated. I was ready to just be single and satisfied with Jesus only.

And of course, God desires that I get married with the right frame of mind and wholeness of spirit.

However, I have to decide.

I have to decide what exactly I want. I have to decide the change I desire to have. I have to decide whether to trust God or keep doing things my way.

Two days ago, I felt starved of men. I felt starved because I have had no calls or texts from any man (non-platonic relationships). I panicked. I didn't realize I was somewhat addicted to talking and chatting with guys. It was a point of self-realization. The issue wasn't just the interaction with men, it was a matter of self-identity and awareness.

So I told God to fix me. I believe He did.

Today, I was faced with temptations. Two of them suddenly wanted to hook up with me. They called. I became afraid.

The temptation was so real.

"You can't keep doing the same thing and expecting a different result," the voice within whispered.

I knew I had to choose. It was about time I made up my mind.

My phone kept ringing. I wanted to switch it off, but something held me back. Switching it off would mean running away from the battle.

I didn't have to run. I had to fight!

As he kept calling, I sang Donnie Mcclurkin's Caribbean Medley:

I've got my mind made up and I won't turn back
Because I want to see my Jesus someday
I've got my mind made up and I won't turn back
Because I want to see my Jesus someday

Goodbye world, I stay no longer with you
Goodbye pleasures of sin, I stay no longer with you
I've made up my mind to go God's way the rest of my life
I've made up my mind to go God's way the rest of my life

Born, born, born again Thank God, I'm born again
Born, born, born again Thank God, I'm born again
Born of the water, spirit and the blood
Thank God, I'm born again
Born of the water, spirit and the blood
Thank God, I'm born again

"It is over. Stop disturbing me!" I spoke. I decreed. I commanded.

I told the devil, "You have failed this time!"

"No man is worth giving up God's glory in my life. I know staying away from men for 30 days is a cross I have to bear. So I am staying focused on seeing a change in my life!"

Some things aren't just worth the energy we exert. Let's take a break. Let's break away to get our breakthroughs.

"Lay aside every encumbrance and sin which do easily entangles us, and let's run with endurance the race that's set before us, fixing our eyes on Jesus."

30 days isn't enough time to make all the changes I want to see in my life but it was a great start. Some days were painful. Some days were relaxing. Some days were challenging. But it was worth it!

* * *

I surrendered my life and love completely to God. I threw myself into Him. I loved Him, still love Him with everything in me. He filled me up. He became enough for me. I didn't need any man to make me feel complete, happy and fulfilled. . . And He prepared me to become an answer to Kachi's prayers.

PART FOUR
Letters

Nwamaka Onyekachi
@Amakamedia

My past - Jesus (He was)
My present - Jesus (He is)
My future - Jesus (He is to come)
#PerfectLife

9:12 PM · 15 Jul 15 · Twitter for Android

CHAPTER THIRTEEN

Letters from God

"I've got a river of life flowing out of me. Spring up, oh well. Spring up."
– Songs and Hymns

In My Season Of Brokenness

With tears in my eyes, I looked up to heaven. I had so much on my mind but didn't say a word. "Jerry never wrote you love letters. Did he?" God teased me. Then He handed me an envelope. It was not the usual I've always known – brown in colour. It was bright, bold and beautiful. I was so excited. I couldn't wait to open it. I admired the envelope for a few seconds and boom! It was a love letter.

My Sweetheart,

I hear you. I hear your lonely calls. I hear you when you speak to Me of heartbreak. I hear you when you speak to Me of pain. My sweetheart, I hear you from the depths of your heart.

I am standing beside you, and holding your hands. I am kneeling before you, and catching your tears. I am holding you. I am here.

Sweetheart, speak to Me. Speak to Me freely. Speak to Me not as though I am far away, but speak to Me as your Love, and speak to Me knowing that you are My love. I am not a psychologist whose job is to listen to you. I am not a priest behind a confession screen, one who doesn't know you, or care to. I am not a parent who doesn't understand. I am not a God far away. I am here.

Sweetie, be open so that I can help you. I always hear your heart, but when you do not speak to Me about what you are feeling, that is when you feel unheard, depressed, and alone. I do not want to see you feel alone. Tell Me how you feel, express your anger, and your desperation. Not only can I heal you of your heartbreak, but I can also help you to power up your feelings with love to inspire the world.

My very own sweet and beautiful Amaka. Always remember I love you whether you love Me right back or not. I do long for your love, but it does not stop Me from loving you. My love does not grow weary like your human love. The love of the flesh cannot endure like My love can.

Come. Come to me so I can drown you and lavish you with love. This is what I do.

Come.

Love,
God.

So it dawned on me that God and I have something in common — writing. I wrote more letters.

My Reply Letter to God

Dear Heart Keeper,

How are You? Me, I feel emotionally exhausted. It's taking a toll on my physical well-being. I've never experienced this much stress, worry, and depression in my life. I know I should have gotten over these feelings by now. It's just hard to let it go.

It's time I went on with my life. Jerry has. I need to stop replaying the memories in my mind. I need to stop memorializing past pains. It's virtually impossible to drive forward and look backward, but that's what I am doing.

It's time for me to relinquish past hurt and the power that has held me prisoner. It's time to forgive myself so I can take hold of the realities that can only be found by walking hand in hand with You to fulfilling purpose.

Heart Keeper, I do not want to oversleep in my past and miss what You have awakened me for. Heal me completely and make me whole.

Love,
Amaka

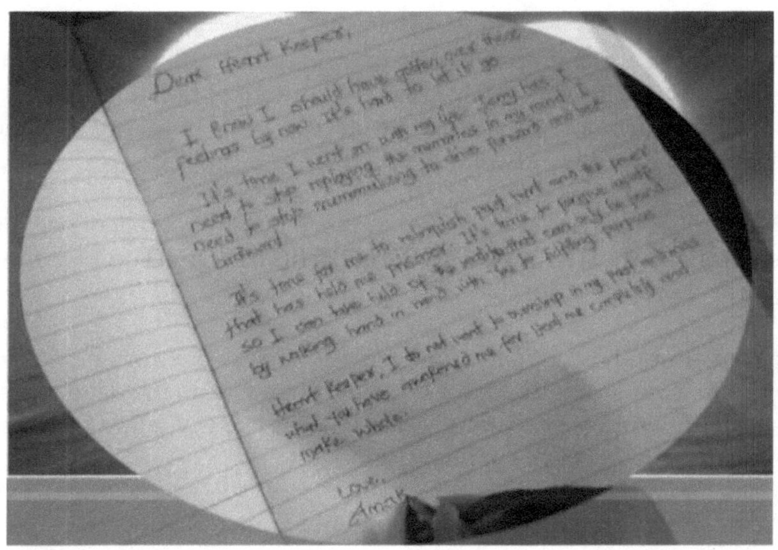

When I Received My Freedom

Me: *closes eyes to pray with tears in her eyes*

I have come on the wings of the wind to meet with You, My heart is aching, longing, desiring. My very being yearns to commune. Oh, how I have missed you, Lord . . .

God: You are no longer held captive in a cocoon, no longer hidden. It is time to fly with freedom under the protection of My mighty wings as you rise to see My face, as it flows with goodness and glory.

Me: I don't know why this keeps happening . . .

God: Awakening is here. Love is awakened, My beloved, swinging wide the doors of opportunity, favour, mercy, glory and honour. Embrace it.

Me: I embrace this day with a great expectation. The expectation to become all I was created to be. The very nature of who You made me is awakening like the rising of the dawn. I have a strong feeling that something massive is about to happen.

God: Your expectations will not be cut short. I am returning hundredfold everything that was stolen while you slept. I will do for you far more abundantly beyond all that you ask or imagine according to your inner power.

In My eyes, you are as graceful and colourful as butterflies drinking pollen from the beautiful flowers of My creation. Fluttering, floating without care, causing amazement as you move from place to place with elegance and grace. You are full of beauty and strength. . .

Me: Me? Full of strength? No, I fell into the temptation. I failed You. I got carried away by the sugar-coated offerings of the enemy, and I let down my guards. Lord, I am not that strong.

God: Your strength is not dependent on your desire or effort, but on My mercy. I am Your strength. I have removed shame from the deep places of your heart. The things you thought and used as excuses, allowing them to bind you in a cocoon of sleep, I have removed.

Me: *tears* How can you love me beyond my faults? No one loves me like this. *

God: You are as beautiful as a butterfly. I have always loved you. I have been jealous for you, My beloved. The things you do can neither increase nor decrease My love for you. I have taken the crooked staff the enemy used to reach out and wrap around your neck, pulling you back into the places of darkness, and turned it into a sword of the Spirit. As you remain faithful to Me, I deny him any power over you. My grace is sufficient, and My love gives you freedom to lift your graceful, yet powerful, wings, so you can soar above all that was.

Me: *tears, tears and more tears* Lord, You are so so faithful . . .

God: All those who discounted you will see you in a new light as I expose you into My promises and the redemption of your calling. Those who cursed you will rise and call you blessed, considering it a privilege to know you.

Me: Amen. Amen. I love You . . . I love You. Keep my heart ever close to You.

God: As you rise and fly in the current of My mighty wings, you will have sight into My realm of goodness and glory. Your perception into things will be Mine. I have called you to collect pollen and take it from place to place. The deposits you share will make it possible for gardens to bloom in the lives of others.

Without pollen, without the deposits of My sweet presence, many would stay in their bound up shells way past the necessary time. The right amount of time produces one like you, while excessive time destroys hope. As you dispense the sweet pollen of My nectar into the lives of others, low self-esteem and self-pity will be exposed and removed, and I will remove the reproach of men upon their lives.

Me: Amen. Amen. Amen.

God: What I do, no one can contend with. Through you, I will remove and break away all words and judgments of men and even families. In the process, I will bring a work of humility to their lives, thereby, freeing them at the same time. In the long run, what I do through you becomes their freedom.

Drink continually in your communion with Me that you may come in and go out of My presence with the necessary pollen to produce in like kind.

Me: Your presence is where I always want to be!

God: I love you, my colourful butterfly.

Me: I fly into my purpose and destiny in the name of Jesus!

When He Brought Me Into The Season Of Release

Today I am breaking the strong gates of iron that have been over you. I am bringing release from the hand of the oppressor. No longer shall you be stolen from or overpowered, for now I have come with My strong hand to rid you of the giants in your land.

I have called you to rise to the occasion and walk in My freedom. Walk in the Jubilee season for what has held you back has been destroyed. You have My anointing that has broken the yoke of the enemy. No longer shall you groan under the spirit of heaviness for I have released My Joy over you. Rejoice, even shout for joy, for I have overcome all your trials and all that has beset you and I have given you the victory.

As you stand in My authority and walk in My presence, you will see the dark clouds of discouragement and despair dissipate as My Son (Sun) shines upon you. Along with My Son, I am raining down My Holy Spirit afresh upon You to give you a season of refreshing.

You have been in the desert where you have been tried and tested by My Spirit. You have come to know that it is not by might nor power but only by My Spirit that you can live, breathe and have your being. You have by experience come to know My Spirit as your Sustainer and your source of Strength. That I AM your Provision. That I AM your Everything. Yes, you have come to understand the concept of Me being the vine and you being the branch and the fact that without Me, you are disconnected and without stable ground. It has not been easy but I have led you by My wisdom as you simply trusted in My ability to lead you day by day.

You are now coming to a season of abundance both spiritually and physically, yet My beloved, the principle of complete trust in Me is still important. The enemy may want to distract you and lead you into passivity while he plunders you, yet I will call you to be alert concerning his wiles. As you remain in Me and allow Me to be your source, I will lead you to your abundance and give you wisdom. I will open your eyes to what the enemy is doing so that you pray accordingly and take action. For indeed, this is a season of abundance, an expansion and an explosion of more. It is also a season that I am training you to war in the Spirit on a higher level than you have known.

Be ready! Be strong and courageous and do not lose sight of the vision. In all your endeavours, I am with you, guiding you by the Holy Spirit if you will listen to My voice and take heed. Great things are coming for you. Great things.

CHAPTER FOURTEEN

Letter To My ~~Future~~ Husband

"I am my beloved's and my beloved is mine"
- Songs of Solomon 6:3, NIV

My Love,
I loved you before I met you. And I will love you unconditionally, here, now, and after.

You are my own. My very own! Wait, are you really mine? I cannot very well take possession of what I am given over heart and soul out of your own possession. It is useless to say you are my own. That's less absolute, because I am yours. So much yours!

I mean, I have your rib! In fact, I am your rib!

And yet, as true as that is, it is not so true. Have you even noticed that your rib is missing?

This might seem like your first letter from me; but it is not the first I have written to you. There are letters to you lying somewhere in a street-seller's shop in this same handwriting — so many, my memory has lost count of them! I wrote to you as though you were going to read them when you find me. I told you about my struggles, passions, day's events, favourite highlights. . . I just unloaded. It was a way for you in the future to glimpse my past. To see my heart before we ever met. To hear about how God's been working and orchestrating all this time. It was going to be a beautiful collection until it became a messy folder and I had to do away with them. But I never stopped writing to you.

As you can see, you are probably reading this one now.

Every time I feel our connection strongly, I close my eyes and pray for you. I have loved and passionately prayed for you in private and (in public). It's one of my favourite things to do. This is how I pray:

My love,
I pray for you . . .
May God give you vision and clarity of purpose.

May His grace and glory be upon you. I pray that you will be passionate about God - loving and knowing Him every day so that you can have a selfless, unashamed boldness that can only come from Him.

My love,
I pray for you . . .
You will learn through day to day experiences and trials how to be a good leader. I pray that you will learn the qualities needed to make a great leader for our family. May you learn integrity, humility, honesty, and above all, love.

My love,
I pray for you . . .
You will make the right choices and decisions. You will succeed. You will make progress. You will fulfill purpose.

My love,
I pray for you . . .
May God give you peace and rest. May you keep your eyes on Him and experience His presence in a whole new way.

My love,
I pray for you . . .
May you stand firm in Christ. May God give you grace to be a light shining in this dark world.

See, we have so many lands to conquer together. You have to be strong for me. Don't let the troubles of life or this world weigh you down. Wherever you are right now, you shall find peace, joy and laughter. I know because I am praying for you.

Most of my friends have already found love, but I'm still waiting for you. Six years ago, I caught the bouquet in a wedding — in fact it more or less fell in my hands — and since then I've stood in thirteen weddings and attended probably a dozen more, all while wondering where you were.

I've been thinking about you so much lately. *Where will we meet? When will it finally happen? Will I just know, or will it take time for me to warm up to you?* Are you wondering these things right now, too?

Oh, I can't wait to meet you!

I have a confession though: I've dated a couple of guys. They were nice and cute, but all they've done so far is point me to the kind of man I'm really looking for. I'm grateful for what I've learned from them. And I'm grateful for the opportunities they provided for me to prepare myself for you.

My love, please. Please get rid of all the distractions in your life, especially girls. Maybe you're with someone right now. I pray for her, that she holds your heart with honour and prays for her future husband the way I pray for you. I hope she teaches you things about yourself that bring you closer to me. I hope you treat her like the image-bearer of God that she is.

I want you to spend time exploring God's truth and trying out new things. Please learn to live your life to the fullest. Live life creatively in the image of God, so we can teach our children, when they come, to do the same.

Guess what? You don't need to prove anything to me, you don't even need to pursue me, PURSUE GOD. Pursue my Creator, Protector, Heart-Keeper and Father. Love Him more than anything else, and at the right time, ask Him for my heart.

See, my love, if you're reading this right now, I honestly can't give you even a single space in my heart. Currently, this heart is totally turned to God. I would have to get an approval from Him. You need to be a man (no one wants to babysit a boy) and personally, I want a man who will be a role model to younger people. One day, my female mentees will be courted and I want them to look at you as an example of someone worth spending a lifetime with.

When I think about my future with you, my stomach fills with all the good types of butterflies. I can't wait to start an amazing family with you. I am so in love with you.

Ah, I love you!
I love your eyes, your lips, your soul, your heart and everything about you.

The truthfulness in your eyes attracts me to you.
The beauty in your soul makes me say I do over again.

Your divine wisdom and loving nature make me want to spend a lifetime with you.

Your attentiveness and your listening ears make you my safe haven.
Your fight to never give up on me makes me cherish you more than ever.
Your quest to glorify God with our union makes me choose you over and
over again.

Your love for God — the One you've never seen — makes me crown you a
king.

Regardless of high times or low times, my love for you shines ever more.
God bless the day we ~~find~~ found each other.

Love,
Your Beautiful ~~Future~~ Wife.

Nwamaka Onyekachi
@Amakamedia

One of the things my children would be able to say is, "mummy was a strong woman."

1:53 PM · 04 Apr 18 · Twitter Web Client

CHAPTER FIFTEEN

Letter To My Future Son

"Things in the past. Things yet unseen. Wishes and dreams. All of my hopes. And all of my plans. And all of my dreams that are yet to come true. My heart and my hands are lifted to You."
- Don Moen

Son,
Sometimes, I wonder what it will be like to hold you and just stare at you for hours. I even wonder if I'd still look pretty carrying you in my womb before then. I know I'll be different when you come along. I am too excited about you.

Yesterday, I was daydreaming and wondering what you will look like. Maybe you'll be chubby. Maybe you'll have full hair. Maybe you'll be dark and tall. Maybe you'll like to sing. Maybe you'll like to write. Either way — you are going to be a very smart guy. I just know it.

It is my desire to raise sons, whose sisters, wives and children would be proud of. It is my desire to be called blessed for your sake.
You are a blessing. Not just to me, but also to your dad, the family, the church and to the world.

There is a future out there with your name written all over it. Only you can decide if you want to live somebody else's future or if you want to live your own. But I want you to take charge of your life. Though I will train you in the way that you should go, but you will choose how to live your life. You would decide for yourself which path to follow. I want you to be a man who knows what he wants and why he wants what he wants. I want you to stand up for what you believe in.

You are going to make mistakes. In fact, you're going to make a lot of them. And that's good because making mistakes is one way to learn, to grow, to become who you were created to be. Own your mistakes, wear them like trophies. Be quick to amend your ways and apologize when you are wrong. People will love you for it.

Learn to forgive people. Even if they don't deserve it or ask for it. Clear your mind and be conscious of all negative energy.

I pray for you every time I think about you.

I pray that you will develop an eternal perspective and purpose, not a mundane one. I pray that you will set your mind on things above, not just what's going on here (on Earth). I pray that you will be rooted and grounded in love. True love.

Love completely. Don't lose sense of your true self to conform or try to be what other people want you to be. God loves you, no matter what. Stay true and always love and serve Him.

You don't need to oversexualize yourself to get attention from girls. Show your heart, show your passions, show your personality – these will bring you the right attention.

Read more books that will benefit your self-growth and add value to your life. Never neglect the Bible. Stay in God.

My boy, I love you just as you are. Always be you.

You know you're amazing, right? I am super proud of you and honoured to have you as a son.

With much love and hope for your bright future,

Mum.

*This page would have been **CHAPTER SIXTEEN: Letter to my Future daughter**...*

But I figured the entire pages of this book is somewhat a letter to her. This is the same story I will tell my daughter someday. What I'll tell her when she comes home crying with a broken heart. I'll tell her of the boys I knew. Of all the boys I once loved. I'll hold her as she whispers the same words that dripped from my own mouth many years before. I'll listen as she tells me about a boy, a boy who promised her the world and then walked away.

HWMH is a story I will tell my daughter when I find her in bed crying over a boy who doesn't deserve her tears. I'll tell her about how it gets better; how each day hurts less than the last until finally she doesn't feel it anymore. I'll tell her about the days she has to look forward to, the days where she will smile again and love again.

This is a story I will tell my daughter when I try to teach her about self-love. When I try to teach her the importance of learning to love herself before loving anyone else. I'll tell her about a girl who lost herself in love only to fall to the deepest depths of the ocean before swimming her way back out.

I'll tell her about how one day, she won't think about that boy anymore.

I'll tell my daughter this story when she meets a guy like Ben, Chidi, Jerry, Enitan or Farouq. I will tell her all these. And more.

Oh, wait. Maybe she wouldn't have to even go through this path. No, she wouldn't. She will know better, act wiser and love more intentionally because I have already gone through this for her.

Dear Future Daughter,

I am convinced you will not see marriage as the ultimate. You will value your relationship with God over all other relationships. You will understand that life is ultimately about finding yourself and fulfilling your purpose. You will understand that marriage is connecting with a good and godly man to share and enjoy the journey of fulfilling purpose with you.

I am convinced that neither death nor life, neither angels nor demons, neither the present nor the future, nor any powers, neither height, nor depth, nor anything else in all creation, will be able to separate you from the love of God that is in Christ Jesus our Lord. (Romans 8:38-39)

Love you,
Mum.

This Page's Not the End

This page is not the end—it is only the beginning of a new chapter. Isn't that exciting? I have much to share still—about love and life and pain and healing. There is no end to this journey. More lessons will continue to unfold and I will grow and grow and grow. . .

But here I feel closure. The closure I've been waiting for. Phew! It's been a liberating cathartic process getting this book out of me.

As Christians, some of us have become experts at putting up a facade of happiness and bliss, pretending that nothing bad ever happens. We assume that if people find out things aren't alright—that our lives are actually chaotic, messy and out of control, relationships are broken, our feelings hurt and we are filled with worry and pain—they'll get scared and run away. So we hide these things with the mistaken belief that we're glorifying God—protecting Him from bad press.

But in doing so, we dishonour God and set ourselves up for failure.

We need to start communicating reality and start owning up to our mistakes, doubts, failures, insecurities and pain. These things are what make us who we are. Let's leave room for being angry, mad, scared, depressed, anxious and broken.

It's healthy to apologize, admit our wrongdoings, and even allow ourselves to question, doubt and change our opinions and beliefs. Let's quit presenting ourselves—and Christianity—as perfect and let's start being genuine. Authentic. Real. Original. Natural. Human!

The reality is, throughout the course of our lives, we'd live through moments; there will be awesome moments and awkward moments, colourful moments and dark moments, memorable moments and regrettable moments. It's wise to experience them all. I collect these moments the way other people save photos or movies. I know that these moments have brought me back to my humanity time and time again, and have connected me to everything I am and all of the things that perhaps I was made for. These mental snapshots make time stand still for all of us, but some people don't even recognize them or realize their significance. Worse, some try to forget these moments happened at all.

Don't lose, forget, or stifle what matters most to you by focusing too much on the same dull, daily routines. They may offer a sense of security and cash but nothing much more. Build your life around experiencing your own "moments" – the ones that will live in your heart forever.

With all these moments come all the emotions that can either stifle us or lend us wings to fly. But whether we stay choked to the past, or soar higher into the future, is dependent on these two poles: Contentment and Gratitude or Bitterness and Unforgiveness.

Forgiveness offers us the option of transforming *bad* memories. It does not take away the memories but it can help remove the sting off them. While gratitude helps to promote the good things that have happened during the course of our lives, un-forgiveness has the ability to magnify our negative experiences. Which would you rather choose?

With forgiveness, we get the opportunity to re-write the impact that our past has on our today.

So now, let me ask you - what makes you think your past doesn't make sense?

I always hear ladies complain about "wasting time" with a guy who didn't marry them. While it may seem like the months or years you spent with a guy who ends up just being another ex is wasted time, that's not necessarily the case. Most guys you meet aren't going to be *The One*, but that doesn't mean meeting and sharing with them has to be a waste of time.

When it comes to love, you're not wasting time — because the only way we can learn about love comes from practice. From actions. From experience.

And love is an experience of a lifetime.

Without these relationship lessons, I don't think I would have been ready to meet my husband, Kachi. My relationships caused me to face anxiety. To stand in the threshold of what I thought was happening and open myself up to see what was actually happening. I would have been immature, naive, impatient, and unprepared and he may have ended up just being another relationship lesson. Thankfully, I was ready to be his wife when our journey to saying "I Do" began.

Relationships form the playground where love, self-esteem, insecurity, worth and value all get to play and help define each other. The sooner you start believing this, the sooner you'll be able to appreciate the process. The moments. The guys. The chapters.

So while it can be tempting to put all our exes in an "ugh" category in our brains — labeling them as "wastes of time" or even unnecessarily taunting ourselves for not seeing the signs sooner — remember that learning to love is a lifelong game that we don't just play with others but with ourselves as well. As we take each relationship for what it is, we will see that the learning that comes from each is invaluable as a mirror to learning about ourselves.

I read somewhere that we live life forward but understand it backward. Perhaps it's hard to make sense of your failed relationship right now, but one day, you will find something to be grateful for, even if it's that you dodged a bullet. So, pick up the pieces of your broken heart, put it back together and look ahead to something better and brighter. Look ahead to the path you're paving towards; your happily ever after and regret nothing.

Regret is the less glamorous side of figuring yourself out and messing up, unfortunately. But for every regret, there's a lesson to take away into your adult life. Yes, that includes all those relationships that didn't lead to marriage.

Instead of trying to understand why it ended, the real question is; *what am I meant to learn?* I've spent much time looking into the past to find answers, only to find that it's better to focus on the lessons in order to move on gracefully to the *promised* future.

So, like me, I think it's time you follow peace with all men. Especially the ones who broke your heart.

One More Thing. . .

If you have visited amakamedia.com recently, you are aware that I enjoy sharing quotes – either written by me, copied from a book, or learnt from someone – to give inspiration. During the course of writing this book, these were some of the quotes I found and needed dearly to keep going. I hope they resonate with you as much as they did with me:

"In the moments you are so weak you feel like stopping, let the hope you have light the road you are walking."
– Heart Rays

"I declare, my past as my strength,
My present as my dedication,
And my future as my inspiration."
– T. D Jakes

"The strongest people help others when they are struggling with theirs."
–Pinterest

"One of the most important moments in life is the moment you finally find the courage to let go of what can't be changed. Because, when you are no longer able to change a situation, you are challenged to change yourself . . . to grow beyond the unchangeable. And that changes everything."
– Unknown

"To be strong, you must be OK with exposing your weakness."
- Hephzibah Frances

"Write your own story. But let God guide the pen when you are writing the story."
– Nwamaka Onyekachi

"Strong women don't play victim, don't make themselves look pitiful, and don't point fingers. They stand and they deal." –Mandy Hale

"To give real service, you must add something which cannot be bought or measured with money, and that is sincerity and integrity."
– Douglas Adams

"To finally move on and start something new, you must release the unchangeable past and embrace your future."
– Nwamaka Onyekachi

God took you from where you used to be because it was not your destination but your transportation."
– T. D Jakes

"Your future will explain your past."
– T. D Jakes

"None of the things that happened to you happened because you are cursed. They happened because you were blessed."
– T. D Jakes

"Everything we thought was possible, is. It just doesn't look like we thought it would look, and it's not in the places we thought it would be. But it's there, it's there."
– Green Roth

"In life, you will realize there is a role for everyone you meet.
Some will use you.
Some love you.
Some will teach you.
But the ones who are truly important are the ones who bring out the best in you."
– Unknown

"You are sent to be a blessing to the world, not to yourself and family alone. You are not a blessing until you start flowing out to others and meeting the needs of the world." – Holy Spirit

"Give it to God, He knows what to do."
– Holy Spirit

"Shh. . .I am writing your love story."
- God

Acknowledgements

Every time I want to write, I ask myself, do I really want to open my heart for the world to see? My words cannot be erased after they are released. And I must confess, it is scary to dangle my feet out here in mid-air. However, I wouldn't fail to show gratitude to a few friends and family members who have been a huge source of support and encouragement.

I'm thrilled to have worked with Ogamars Creatives who thought about this lovely cover design. They also designed my wedding invitation cards. How beautiful God works. Thank you, Ogamars.

Many thanks to Ify Halim for her editorial dexterity. She wanted this book and fought hard to get it. I'm grateful for her push and enthusiasm. Thank you, Ify.

To The Women At The Well (TWTW), thank you for being my girliest of all girlfriends and providing a place where truth is always honoured and courage is built for women to own and share their stories. To The Amplify Network, thank you for the moral support and showing how much you believe in me. And to every single person who has taken out time to encourage me on this path of mine, you know yourselves, thank you.

I would love to thank my amazing blog readers. Oh my sweethearts, may you be blessed and may you never lack people to lean on. There were times when words couldn't do justice to what I felt in my heart, yet you understood and stood by me. Thank you.

Ah, God, my Heavenly Father, my Heart Keeper, the Lifter of my head. You simply take my breath away. Thank You for loving me first and doing it so lavishly. Keep blowing my mind, Lord!

Finally — please forgive me if I get mushy — Kachi, my love, Dim oma, I'm forever grateful for you. This book would have remained as an unfinished draft if it wasn't for your daily encouragement. Thank you for showing up at the perfect time, loving me all the way and calling it "our book". The story continues!

**THIS IS MORE THAN JUST A BOOK.
IT'S A MOVEMENT.**

DON'T JUST READ IT, LIVE IT OUT.

Make sense out of the true love stories from your past and use it to inspire another.

Join the conversation on Twitter, Instagram, Facebook and Nwamaka Onyekachi's blog and let's start a movement. Use the hashtag #HeWasntMyHusband

Facebook:
Facebook.com/Amakamedia

Twitter:
twitter.com/Amakamedia

Instagram:
Instagram.com/Amakamedia

Blog:
Amakamedia.com

Let's do this!

About The Author

NWAMAKA ONYEKACHI is a lover of creative expressions. She manages public relations for corporate brands and creates masterpieces for radio,TV, social media and print. She is a lifestyle blogger, voice-over artist and an inspirational/relationship speaker.

Her unique gift lies in her ability to speak honestly and intimately of her own experiences, in her devotion to the craft of writing and to making sense of the world in new and inspiring ways. *He Wasn't My Husband* recounts her further journey into the recesses of her own heart, and offers insight into the journey of love, intimacy, healing, wholeness, and genuine joy and peace. She is happily married to the man of her dreams.

Check out her love for Ankara designs on @amakaankara (Instagram) or catch up on her musings on life at www.amakamedia.com.